CROFTS AND CROFTING

For Bernice,

CROFTS AND CROFTING

KATHARINE STEWART

all good wishes
Katharine Stewart.

mercatpress
www.mercatpress.com

First published in 1980 by William Blackwood
Reprinted in 1990 and 1996 by Mercat Press
This revised and expanded edition published in 2005 by Mercat Press Ltd
10 Coates Cresent, Edinburgh EH3 7AL
www.mercatpress.com

ISBN: 1841830712

Set in Bembo and Benguiat at Mercat Press

Printed in Great Britain by Bell and Bain

CONTENTS

Illustrations

To the people of the crofts,
whose friendship I prize—
agus mo bheannachdan
agus mo mhile taing
dhaibh uile.

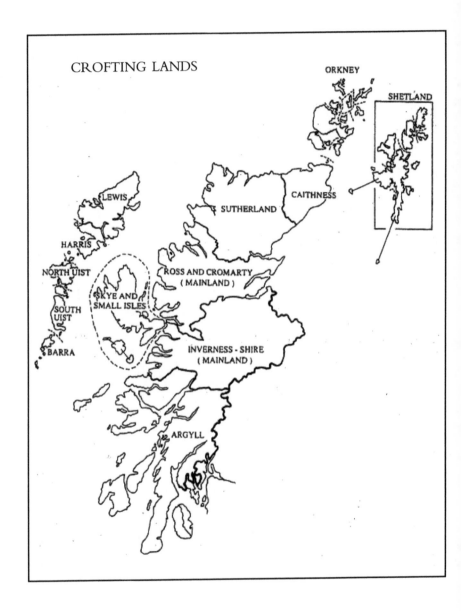

CROFTING LANDS

ORKNEY

SHETLAND

LEWIS

CAITHNESS

HARRIS

SUTHERLAND

NORTH UIST

ROSS AND CROMARTY
(MAINLAND)

SKYE AND
SMALL ISLES

SOUTH
UIST

BARRA

INVERNESS - SHIRE
(MAINLAND)

ARGYLL

INTRODUCTION

I, myself, have had the great good fortune of having worked a croft in a place where, and at a time when, the people who belonged there were living and working as their forebears had for many generations.

The place was an upland area, 800 feet to the north of Loch Ness, known as Caiplich, just up the road from Abriachan. The people were Frasers, Macdonalds, Chisholms, Macleans; all Gaelic speakers and all prepared to give the traditional welcome to strangers.

Those were the days of the ever-open door, the kettle bubbling on the hob to make the 'strupach', the dram in the cupboard for a day of storm. And they were the days of labour shared when the going was hard. An informal squad would turn up, hoes at the ready, when the turnip seedlings were needing to be thinned. Strong arms would appear out of the blue when the oats had to be stacked in the face of approaching rain clouds. At the gathering of the sheep, the dipping and the clipping, six pairs of legs and arms got the job done more quickly and efficiently than two. At the peat-cutting whole families would join forces to make a picnic of the day, up on the scented moor ground, in spite of tired muscles and a plague of infuriating insects!

In times of illness, storm or food shortage, our own small welfare state would come into action, with help on the doorstep within minutes.

And there was time in the evenings, to relax, to discuss the issues of the day and to listen to tales and reminiscences from the lively minds of our neighbours.

Things were moving on, even then. We watched the coming of the electricity on its huge pylons and the telephone cables. Now mains water has arrived. But it hasn't the life force of the liquid from the spring!

Acres of commercial conifers have lately been bought by the community, felled and replaced by native trees. The old peat roads have become paths for leisured tourist feet. Woodland and hillside have been pathed for botanists, birdwatchers, naturalists. For children there is a treehouse, a bird–hide and a school in the forest; a place where they can learn about wildlife and biodiversity while right in among it. There is a sharing, now, of the riches of the hills.

With most people engaged, in varying degrees, in the one enterprise—the forest and its resources—the sense of communal effort is there, and in the sharing of labour and care for the environment, echoes of the old way of life can be heard in the new.

KATHARINE STEWART

1

IN THE BEGINNING

The word 'croft', from the Gaelic 'croit', means a small area of enclosed land. The significance of this derivation becomes clear when considering the ways of holding and working land evolved in what became known as 'the crofting counties', the former counties of Shetland, Orkney, Caithness, Sutherland, Ross and Cromarty, Inverness and Argyll.

In very early times, before the emergence of the clans, there was a belief that lengthy occupation of land gave right to what was called a 'kindness' or permanency of settlement, though not actual ownership, of that land. This belief persisted into later ages. The Royal Commission appointed in 1883 to enquire into crofting said in its report: 'This opinion was often expressed before us—that the small tenantry of the Highlands have an inherited inalienable title to security of tenure in their possessions while rent and service are duly rendered is an impression indigenous to the country, though it has never been sanctioned by legal recognition and has long been repudiated by the action of the proprietors.'

Also from those early days dates the belief that the Highlander has the right to take 'a stag from the hill, a salmon from the pool and a tree from the wood', an idea which dies hard.

A feeling of close affinity with the natural world is a mark of the Celt. An early Irish poet said:

I am the wind which breathes upon the sea,
I am the wave of the ocean,
I am the murmur of the billows,
I am a powerful ox,
I am a hawk on a cliff,
I am a beam of the sun,
I am the fairest of the plants,
I am a wild boar in valour,
I am a salmon in a pool,
I am a lake in a plain,
I am a word of science,
I am a lance point in a battle,
I create in man the fire of thought.

The power of observation of the natural world finds expression in the marvellous fertility of the Gaelic language which has, for example, over a dozen different words for an area of high ground; the territory most familiar to the people, according to whether it rises sharply and is high, is rounded, is less high and is pointed, or is a small hillock, a longer slope, is rocky and steep, or rocky and flat. There are many more. This feeling of affinity persists. Exiles travel from the furthest corners of the world to see the places so graphically named—'the cold, wet hill', 'the loch of the white eagle'—by their forebears. Often they will take back a stone, a piece of peat, even a small bag of earth from the place that was once home. The sense of belonging is indestructible. It means identity.

A look at history will tell how this sense of belonging persisted through the ages, through the creation of crofts and its aftermath, and on to today, when new ways of land-holding are coming in to being.

The Celtic people known as Scots came from Ireland, *Erin*, during the fifth century A.D. to settle in the south west, in what is now Argyll, forming a colony, an outpost, which they called *Dalriada*, the name of the place from which they came. They brought with them their 'dualchas', their hereditary culture, their Gaelic language. There were already Celtic people in the Clyde valley, the Britons, while to the north and east the Picts were in control and threatened several times to overrun the small kingdom of the

Scots. But they, as Celts, enjoyed the solidarity of an already sophisticated social system. In their world there was no such concept as absolute ownership of land. When a tribe occupied a territory it belonged to them as a community. Territory was delineated by natural boundaries and divided for the benefit of all. A large section was retained for use as common land. Another part was set aside for the maintenance of the poor, the old, the sick.

In this primitive 'welfare state', those working the land paid taxes for the upkeep of the community as a whole. There was no slavery, there were no prisons. Lawbreakers simply lost civil rights. The 'nobility', a kind of 'civil service', consisted of elected representatives, who administered the decisions of an assembly. They held land in return for seeing to the welfare of all, collecting taxes, keeping roads in repair, and in times of war organizing the army. There were professionals—druids, bards, lawyers, doctors. Poets, story-tellers and minstrels were appreciated and encouraged, all having their valued place, as had the craftsmen who made fabulously beautiful artefacts, many of which have survived. The chieftain was president of the tribal assembly, their military commander and judge. If he failed in his duties he could be replaced. Women had equal rights with men and could become chieftains. The entire tribe lived as a close-knit community. In the year 864 Kenneth Macalpine, a chieftain who had become a high king of the Scots, succeeded to the throne of the Picts, and the kingdom of Alba, as Scotland was then known, was born.

At this time the Norsemen, the Vikings, were conquering and settling in many parts of the island and the mainland. Place-names of Norse origin remain. But the Norsemen were not as culturally advanced as the Gaels and did not succeed in obliterating Celtic civilisation.

The Gaelic kingdom, with its old Celtic way of life, survived, but under the rule of Malcolm Canmore and his successors (1057–1289), influences from the south became important and the social structure of Scotland was drastically changed as the feudal system of landholding was introduced. Large grants of land were made to incomers from the south, many of them of Norman origin. A new concept of the legal right to ownership of land developed. Power was the deciding factor. The king was considered the owner of the land with the right to grant lots by charter to certain subjects in return for dues, including military service. A 'Barony', for instance, was the amount of land expected to provide the service of an armed and mounted 'baron'. After the Wars of Independence which Scotland waged against England between 1296 and 1314 much land held by English sympathisers was made forfeit and re-allocated to Scottish patriots. This was an important factor in the growth of the clan society.

The word 'clan' is from the Gaelic 'clann', meaning children. This makes clear the relationship between a chief and his followers. He looked upon his clansmen as members of his family, often fostering a son of his with a clansman in order to seal the relationship. Each member of the clan claimed kinship with the chief, who provided protection, administered justice and cared for the dependants of those who had given good service. The old Celtic ways were surviving. It was, if you like, an aristocratic society, the lowliest member of the clan sharing the dignity and bearing of those closest to the chief. The sense of underlying kinship gave the people confidence to endure the hardships of their daily lives, or of time spent in combat when called upon by their chief.

Life for the chief, though not in most cases lavish, was enhanced by the establishment of an entourage which included a bard—a poet and recorder of clan history—who would compose praise poems in his honour. These bards would undergo a rigorous training, attending 'bardic schools'. The talent for composing poems and songs was inherent in the people. The chief had also a piper, an entertainer, and on forays abroad, a sword-bearer, a ferryman, and other attendants to make his going easier. Evenings would be pleasant times of relaxation. On occasion clansmen would join the long table to share the meal and the drink—wine, whisky or ale. As inter-clan warfare developed it was in the interests of the chief to have a large following. Gradually the clan was extended to include all who would acknowledge the authority of a particular chief. Sometimes, after a battle decimated the ranks of a certain clan, attempts would be made to persuade members of a neighbouring clan to swap allegiance. In one instance, a Fraser of Lovat offered the inducement of a 'boll' of meal to any who would adopt his name. Those who accepted came to be known as 'Boll o' Meal' Frasers.

By the seventeenth century, when clan territories were fairly well established, a chief would give a permanent lease of land to a son or other close relative, who became known as a 'tacksman', that is, a receiver of rent. These tacksmen were responsible for the military organisation of the clan. They would sublet parts of their land in return for services and produce. Later, many of them were to seek their fortune abroad.

The people in these times, from the sixteenth to the eighteenth centuries, were living in townships, groups of small houses, with the adjoining portion of arable land worked in common, in strips, which were balloted each year, so that everyone had a share in the better and poorer ground. This was known as the run–rig system. It was essentially a democratic way of working and led to much communal activity, at times of sowing or reaping. The work was hard with the tools available at the time—the 'cas-chrom' or foot-plough and the sickle. The labour was often lightened by the singing of songs, which kept the rhythm going. Wordsworth, on his visit to the Highlands, tells in his famous poem how he heard the 'Highland lass' singing at her work.

The people elected a 'constable' who saw to the allocation of the land. To show his commitment to the job he would stand in his bare feet, with a lump of earth on his head. He was, himself, part of the land, as the poet Amergin would have said. He also allocated the peat-banks, saw to the making of the peat-road, and worked out the 'souming', that is the number of cattle each household was entitled to put on the common grazing. In return for this work he was given the right to use the grazing. The people would meet regularly, at a certain rock or hillock, to discuss the affairs of the township. It was a close-knit, communal life.

The crops grown were oats, bere (a primitive form of barley) and grass for hay. Potatoes and turnips were not introduced until the eighteenth century. The people kept a few sheep, near the door, for the production of wool for clothing and for their milk. Goats were also kept and some poultry. But the mainstay of the community was the raising of cattle. The whole year revolved around seeing to the welfare of the cattle. The feast of Beltane, the fire of the sun god, at the beginning of May, was when the cattle were driven through a purifying fire before being driven to the hill. The feast of Samhain, at the end of October, celebrated their return to winter quarters.

For these cattle a large area of hill grazing was essential. They were hardy beasts who could brave the elements most of the year, but during the worst of the winter, they were stalled in one end of the house. A mutual exchange of warmth, human and animal, was welcome. A milking cow supplied a large part of the diet of a family, and her calves, when they matured, provided some income. Sometimes, by spring, the cattle, weakened by scanty feeding, would have to be hauled outside and tended with care till they regained some strength.

2

THE SHIELING

Transhumance, or shifting of livestock to high ground during the summer, is a common practice, still followed today in many parts of Europe. Up until comparatively recently in the Highlands, when the crops were established in the low-ground fields and the peats were cut, the women and the girls, the children and some of the boys would go up with the cattle and a few sheep, perhaps some goats, to the high pastures. The men would go up some days ahead of the main party, in the 'small flitting', to repair the little dwellings which might have been damaged in winter storms. They were simple structures, with walls of stone or turf, heather-thatched, sometimes built on the foundations of an iron-age house. There would be several 'little houses', one set aside for the milk vessels, away from the heat of the cooking fire.

As the time for departure drew near there was great excitement in the community. On the eve of the big day a simple meal was taken in common, with a blessing invoked in the song on the cattle. One such song, collected by Alexander Carmichael, is known as 'Columba's Herding':

> May the herding of Columba,
> Encompass you going and returning,
> Encompass you in straight and in ridge,
> And on the edge of each rough region.
> May it keep you from pit and from mire,

> Keep you from hill and from crag,
> Keep you from loch and from downfall,
> Each evening and each darkling.
> The peace of Columba be yours in the grazing,
> The peace of Brigit be yours in the grazing,
> The peace of Mary be yours in the grazing,
> And may you return home safe-guarded.

On the day of the 'big flitting' it was a noisy setting-off, the children laughing and shouting, dogs barking, cattle lowing, sheep scattering. Ponies and vehicles—carts, sledges, lobans—were laden with milk vessels, cheese presses, pots, meal bags, spindles, spinning wheels, flax, wool, blankets, clothing, dry peats for the fire. Some shieling were quite far from the home ground, some fairly near. A few were known by the names of saints and might have been places of retreat in the days of the early Celtic church.

In most cases the trek would take the best part of the day. The men in the advance party would have stacked some peat and gathered heather for bedding. As soon as the unloading was done, the women and girls would get busy at milking the cows on the green near the dwellings, sometimes with the animals back legs tied together to keep them steady. The girls would have favourites among the cows, giving them names, knowing each one's ways and singing to them as they drew the milk:

> Lovely black cow, pride of the shieling,
> First cow of the byre, choice mother of calves,
> Wisps of straw round the cows on the townland,
> A shackle of silk on my heifer beloved,
> Ho, my heifer, ho my gentle heifer.

Goats would be milked, their milk much prized as health-giving. Sheep's milk was also used in the making of cheese. Large quantities of superb butter and cheese were made over the summer. Some would be sent down to the men at home, some preserved in kegs buried in the peat. A form of milkshake was made by frothing up a cup of milk with a special little plunger. This was much relished by the children.

The boys would herd the cattle all day, bringing them into a field near the houses at night. To pass the time herding they would gather herbs or carve, with just a sharp knife, spirtles or cogs for holding milk. They would also provide for the larder, with a surreptitious shot at a young roe, a rabbit snared, trout guddled in the burn.

The girls learnt all the dairying skills, as well as the skills of spinning. Flax, for the making of linen, was often spun at the shieling. The thread is fine and the summer light helps in the working of it. The women knew the lichens and roots used for dyeing the wool and would pass on this knowledge to the younger generation, girls and boys. Bunches of myrtle were gathered to keep the flies away in the dairy.

Life at the shieling was a busy time but essentially a happy one. Songs were made and sung as the work went on. And there were love songs, too, as the herd boys cast eyes at the dairy-maids.

> Brown-haired girl I would choose you,
> Ho-ro you would be my choice.
> Brown-haired girl I would choose you,
> For sweetness and for beauty.
> Brown-haired girl of the fold,
> Young did I give you my devotion.
> No other shall take you from me,
> Unless he wins you with gold.

And there was dancing on the green in the long summer evenings.

Meanwhile the men, back at the home ground, were also busily employed and enjoying many a ceilidh together, with a smoke and a dram. Some would take the opportunity to rethatch the house. The old thatch, impregnated with reek from the peat fire, made valuable fertiliser and would be ploughed into the arable plots in the spring. Some men would tan hides to make brogues for the winter. Others were skilled weavers or tailors and would get on with this work while the crops were ripening.

Towards the end of the summer, when the hill grass was losing its sap, there would be a move home from the shieling, with the cattle fat and glossy, some of them ready for the long drive to the autumn markets in the south. The children were glowing with health after the long days in the hill air and an ample diet of fresh food.

The homecoming was celebrated with great rejoicing, everyone in good heart and ready to tackle the next big job—the harvest. This meant life for the people and for their precious cattle through the winter ahead.

Sadly, little trace can now be found of these shieling that were once so full of life. The small dwellings have weathered away. But patches of bright green sward on the hillsides still mark the spots where the cattle grazed. Only in some parts of the Isle of Lewis do the people still go up to the shieling. The songs remain:

> Brown-haired lass of the shieling,
> I would surely sit with you,
> On the top of the high hills,
> And on the shieling of the hillocks.

Sung at the winter ceilidh this can conjure up the magic of the long summer days.

3

CHANGING TIMES

In the course of the eighteenth century, after the union of the Scottish and English parliaments, communication with the south began to develop more widely. General Wade was sent up to investigate conditions in the Highlands to discover what irked the hereditary chiefs, driving them to the point of rebellion. His first report indicated that the lack of internal communication facilities was the most important factor in keeping the area a fastness, where it was difficult to maintain law and order. Even tracks were non-existent over the vast acreages of hill and moor. So began a huge programme of work building bridges and roads, many of which remain today.

Easier access to the south opened up opportunities of many kinds. The chiefs began to absent themselves more frequently from their lands, no longer as soldiers fighting European wars, but as seekers after the more leisurely life enjoyed by their counterparts in the south. This lifestyle demanded money which they, as clan patriarchs, found difficulty in raising. Large debts were incurred. The chiefs were obliged to consider ways of making their lands profitable. After the defeat of the Jacobites at Culloden in 1746 the destruction of the clan as a military organisation, threatening the stability of the state was inevitable. The carrying of guns, the playing of pipes, the wearing of traditional garb were all forbidden under penalty of imprisonment or deportation. This was followed by various attempts to 'modernise' the Highland economy.

Modernisation meant supplying the needs of the developing industries of England and lowland Scotland. Cattle had always been the traditional export of the Highlands. Now it was discovered that two other commodities could be produced—wool and kelp. The money economy had arrived.

The southern mills needed large supplies of wool, much of it used in the making of uniforms for the army. Wool meant sheep. With his former clansmen, now known primarily as tenants, unable to pay him an adequate rent, the chief, now becoming known as the laird, was obliged to evict many of them to make way for incoming sheep-farmers from the south. These men needed large acreages for their flocks and were able to pay a substantial rent. Houses were built for them, good stone houses built with lime and known as the 'white' houses, with roofs of slate. Some of these houses remain and the names of their former occupants are still known. The coming of the big sheep—*na caoraich mora*—was a time of great distress for the people. Evictions were carried out all over the Highlands and the Islands, some with great cruelty. People for whom their chief had traditionally represented fair-minded justice, protection, help in time of need, found it impossible to believe what was happening to them. As the reality grew, bitterness was born. Anger would ensue.

Roofs were set on fire to make the little houses uninhabitable. Old people and children were left to shelter in the lea of stone dykes while the active members of the family sought desperately to find a lodging. There was word of emigration, but very few could raise the money for the fare. Some lairds provided ships, forcing people on board, and sailing to emerging colonies in Canada, Australia, New Zealand. Conditions on board were so appalling that many people died on the voyage. On arrival they found new difficulties—impenetrable forest or bleak desert, hostile natives, strange animal and plant life.

In 1841 Robert MacDougall published *The Emigrants' Guide to North America*. Written in Gaelic, in a lively style, it draws upon the author's own experience of life in upper Canada, as he says: 'For I was there and I saw it.'

He gives practical advice on what the emigrant should take in the way of clothing, household untensils, bedding, even food. He insists on the importance of having ministers of religion and teachers among the 'flock'. He warns against the cold, saying 'I have no words to describe its harshness as, in truth, the Gaelic language is not capable of describing it and, since it is not, I have given up hope that there is any other language that can.'

He gives advice on felling trees and on planting, also on 'the making of sugar'. Canada, at this time, was known as the 'land of trees and sugar'. He tells of the dangers of encountering wildlife, including mosquitoes and gadflies! He himself stayed only three years in Canada, then went to Australia. Perhaps the Canadian cold was too much for him!

Those who did not emigrate were cleared to unproductive parts, marginal land or to the coast. They were given a small holding of enclosed land, with a share in some common grazing: a croft.

4

THE CROFTS

Small houses on rough stone foundations with walls of turf, thatched roofs and perhaps a lining of wicker were quickly put up. Some families were allowed to take their 'roof-tree', the most precious commodity in a barren land. The small, close-knit communities, living as they had done for centuries, were now scattered into isolated units.

The acreage of the croft was deliberately kept low so that the occupant could engage in other work, work of benefit to the landlord. People whose ancestors had always lived in sheltered glens were expected to adapt to life on a small plot of land on a storm-swept coast. It was hard for those who had never set eyes on the sea. There was certainly the chance to make a small wage working in the kelp industry: that is, the burning of seaweed to produce alginate, a substance used in the manufacture of glass and soap. It was seasonal work, the weed being gathered at low tide in the summer, brought ashore and burnt. Twenty tons of weed were needed to produce one ton of ash. A large labour force was employed.

The continuous heavy handling of the material, in wet and often cold conditions, meant that workers suffered sickness of many kinds. For the landowners it was a very profitable business for a good many years during the Napoleonic wars. With the coming of peace barilla was imported from Spain and the trade in kelp collapsed.

The kelp workers were left with no alternative but to hire themselves and members of their families out as harvesters on the big inland farms. Their own small crofts then suffered neglect.

Meanwhile, the fishing industry was being developed with the building of small harbours, known as ports. The fishing was a skilled business and did not initially offer employment to many. There were problems: distance from markets, and lack of salt—the only preservative once the fish left the ice-houses which were being built—meant that much produce was wasted. Sailing rough seas in ramshackle boats was a hazardous business. Some young men were harried by the press gang when out at sea and forced into service in the Navy. Later, seafaring did enter the blood of many. The Merchant Navy beckoned, and islemen in particular became skilled sailors, roaming the 'seven seas'.

In inland areas some landowners, aware of the plight of many of their erstwhile clansmen, set up model villages, where men whose skills had always been part of their everyday life could set themselves up as practitioners of these skills on a profitable footing. They could 'sell' their skills as masons, carpenters, weavers, shoemakers, tailors and so on. This did happen, in Grantown-on-Spey and Milton, in Glen Urquhart. But many did not take easily to a settled, tradesman's life. As Mrs Grant of Laggan, the author of the *Letters from the Mountains*, put it: 'To set a man to a loom is like putting a plough to a deer'. The crofter, as he was now known, preferred to be a Jack-of-all-trades in his own way, on his own place.

With no security of tenure, however, his initiative and enterprise were stifled. Also, if he made improvements by walling, draining or putting up additional buildings, his rent was increased. There was always the army, where Highland recruits were welcome, many having seen service in local militia. To 'take the king's shilling' meant at least food, shelter, clothing and, best of all, a gun in the hand. There was also the possibility of acquiring a share in some of the lands to which they were sent to fight for king and country.

In 1846 the failure of the potato crop, on which so many families had come to depend, caused famine. At last the authorities were forced to recognise the plight of the crofting community and some effort was made to help. Food and work were provided in the making of roads, which are still known as destitution roads and are used today. Some lairds did distribute meal, but the root cause of the trouble was the lack of land to provide food other than potato. The solution was, once again, emigration, and again so many able and enterprising families were lost to the Highlands for good.

Attempts were made by Lord Selkirk and Norman Macleod to have emigrants settling *en masse* in one particular area so that their traditional way of life could be maintained, their working practices, their language, their music, all the facets of their life. Norman Macleod, in particular, who was a religious leader and had sailed from Ullapoool in 1817, did achieve this in Prince Edward Island in Canada, and in Naipu in New Zealand. In these places Gaelic culture has been maintained today. Lord Selkirk's 'Red River Colony', in northern Canda, was not so successful, as the area was marshy and plagued by malarial mosquitoes. He also had problems with the Hudson Bay Company, which was only interested in dealing in furs and did not welcome settlers. He did, however, settle colonists in Prince Edward Island, where their descendants flourish 200 years later.

5

THE SKILLED HANDS

For people living a hard outdoor life, working long hours at all times of the year, a house was essentially a refuge, a place for shelter and warmth. Skills in the building of such a place had been acquired over the centuries. In most parts the material was to hand— stone, turf, wood, heather or rushes. It was reckoned that a house for a newly-married couple could be built in one day by neighbours working together. The design of the structure took account of the elements. In the windswept islands the end walls were rounded to break the force of Atlantic gales. Everywhere, the thatch of heather, rushes or even bracken was held secure by weighted ropes. In the summer the roof often sported a crop of colourful wild flowers! The walls would be several feet thick and often lined with wicker. To step out of a wild storm into such an almost soundless haven produces a feeling of complete security and comfort. The door was low and windows merely apertures which could be closed by the insertion of a block of peat.

Today, planners are looking again at the building methods of older times. At last the inhumanity of living in high-rise blocks is being recognised.

In the Islands young architects are designing houses based on the old logical principles: long, low structures, even with rounded gable-ends to defeat the destructive powers of nature. New inventions such as solar panels in the roof can be adopted without destroying the essentially low impact on the environment. Turf roofs are being added to some existing buildings as a healthy form of insulation; some even support a crop of wild flowers. A sheep can always be borrowed to deal with excessive growth.

In early houses the fire was in the middle of the main room, the smoke escaping by a hole in the thatch. Sometimes smoke came through other parts of the thatch, so that it seemed from outside, that the whole house was smouldering. People sat on low stools to avoid inhaling smoke. They sat, literally, 'round the fire' and usually ate from a dish or bowl on their knee.

Johnson and Boswell, in their account *Journey to the Hebrides* which they took in 1773, each give a description of a house on the shore of Loch Ness, a house typical of the time and of the welcome they received there. These accounts of early travellers are a valuable source of information. Conditions in the houses were cramped, as often three generations would live under the same roof. The older members were much valued for their skilled work of a sedentary nature—spinning, rope and basket-making—and for their care of the younger children. There was always a place for them at 'bed and board', as there was for other family members and for those who 'stopped by'. The door was never fastened. There was a saying:

> I saw a stranger yestreen
> And I have put food in the eating place
> I put drink in the drinking place
> For often, often, often
> Comes the Christ
> In the stranger's guise.

The parents slept in a box bed, a bed enclosed by doors or a curtain, on a mattress of heather. Children could sleep on the 'roof' of the bed and underneath was a storage space. Furnishings were of the simplest kind: chairs made from shaped branches, with a plank for a seat, the whole held together with wooden pegs; a table, a dresser with shelves to hold dishes, perhaps a cupboard with sides made of wicker to keep the contents aired. Plates were of wood, spoons and cups of horn. The most valued household appliance was the cooking pot, made from iron and hung from the rafters on

an iron chain. This replaced the
old wooden chain and would
have to be blacksmith-made, so
was a kind of status symbol. Iron
was always looked on with a
sense almost of awe. Coming out
of the ground and malleable in
heat, there was a touch of magic
about the substance and the
working of it. The blacksmith
himself was highly regarded.

In the disposal of human waste, propriety was always strictly
observed. The women would take themselves to the stable, the
man to the byre end. The Chinese also practised the use of such
waste. In spite of the crowded conditions, and the basic simplicity
of their lifestyle, indeed perhaps because of it, early travellers all
noted the quiet dignity of the people and the readiness of their welcome.

The kist, a wooden chest, held the precious oatmeal, the basis
of the daily diet. In some houses a wooden settle, a boxed seat,
could make storage space for blankets and could accommodate
visitors. In coastal areas for lighting, fish-
oil was used, in cup-shaped, lipped vessels
called 'cruisie lamps', with peeled rushes
for wicks. In landward parts fir-candles
were made from pinewood that had lain
buried in the peat. In later times candles of
mutton fat were cast in tin moulds. The
glowing embers of the peat fire gave light
enough for skilled fingers to engage in the
familiar ploys of spinning, basket-making
or the mending of nets.

The people were adept at making use of the materials they found
to hand. Heather, as well as making thatch and bedding, was also
used to make rope, along with rushes or straw, and to fashion pot-
scrubbers and besoms (brooms). It also made ale. It is said that the
Romans tried in vain to get the recipe for the heather ale, which
they considered made their enemies, the Picts, invincible! Willow

or hazel wands made the traditional wicker lining for the house walls and baskets for many purposes. When so many loads had to be carried by men, women and ponies, these were indispensable. Creels for the human back and panniers for the pony's took many a load of peat from the hill or seaweed from the beach. Wicker sides were sometimes built on to sledges or 'slipes', simple devices of rough wood used to pull loads over the rough ground. Wicker-sided bogies were known as 'lobans' and were in use until quite recently. 'Withies', strands of fine sapling, were used to make the harness for the ponies.

Wicker is being used today to make attractive, unobtrusive fencing in gardens and parks. The skill in making baskets and containers is also being revived. These occupations provide relief from the stress of many other forms of work.

Bracken, also known as 'fern', has been used since prehistoric times as bedding—for humans and animals—floor-covering, insulation and thatching. Later, it could be used to pay rent. In the eighteenth and ninteenth centuries it was burned, as kelp was, to make potash for use in soap and glassmaking. The Native Americans have used bracken for medicinal purposes by cooking the root. In sixteenth century Britain it was made in to treatment for burns, wounds and sores. Today, as it no longer serves any of its former purposes, it has taken over vast areas of the country. The only way of eradication is said to be a thrice-yearly drastic cutting–back.

Footwear was made from hide, tanned in oak sap. These 'brogues' were hard-wearing and waterproof, essential for men taking forays into the hills or journeys to outlying townships. The women and children mostly went barefoot in the summer.

In later times, when men and women had to travel quite far afield to find work to supplement the family income and more footwear was needed, a shoemaker would supply the demand, charging a small price. A place in the hills above Loch Ness is known as the 'Shoemakers', where, it is said, seven plied their trade successfully.

Likewise, with the making of clothing: another specialised craftsman who was supported by the community was the tailor. In this same upland area this fact is commemorated in the name *parc an taillear*—the tailor's field. The tailor would often stay in his customer's house while working, and would be fed and made welcome as a messenger with news and gossip from other parts. The Celtic people had always taken pride in their appearance and, when they could afford to do so, they liked to indulge their love of fine wear. Also, they owed to their women the skills necessary to provide the essential fabric for the tailor. From the earliest times, when the few domestic sheep provided her with wool, the woman of the house would set to work with her spindle.

Winding a piece of fleece round a length of wood—the distaff— she would work it into thread, twist it and feed it in to a dangling piece of wood weighted with a holed stone—the spindle. These spindle stones have been found in prehistoric settlements. This is an ancient craft. To make the yarn was a lengthy business, but the woman could spin while doing some other job, herding the cattle or bringing peat from the hill. When the spinning-wheels came in the women did not take to them at first as it meant the work was sedentary, though it was pleasant on a summer day sitting at the door in the sunshine, or at the fire on a winter evening, with a daughter teasing out the yarn, with a pair of carders.

Much weaving was also done at home, on wooden looms, the men sometimes working them. After taking the web from the loom, further processing was necessary—the shrinking. This was a communal activity, known as 'waulking' the cloth. Perhaps a dozen members would take part, in older times sitting on the ground and working with their feet. Later, it was the custom for them to sit on opposite sides of an improvised table, often a door taken off its hinges for the purpose. The cloth, which had been soaking in urine, was passed sunwise from hand to hand, the women thumping it rhythmically and singing, slowly at first, then working up to an ecstatic crescendo. As this was an all-female activity, many of the songs poked fun at the men and allowed the women to discard their inhibitions! Finally, the cloth was rolled, stretched and rolled again and a blessing was put on it. As with all communal activity a lot of fun ensued, there was much teasing and laughter, with food and drink for everyone before the parting of the ways.

Cloth woven in the Highlands had a special and unique beauty.

The skill of the women, handed down through the centuries, was in finding and using the plants which gave the colours. Lichens gave various shades of brown, lady's bedstraw gave red, black came from the alder or the roots of tormentil, yellow from birch leaves or heather. Dyeing was mostly done outside, on a fire of heather, roots and peat. In a huge iron pot the wool and the dye plant, with 'mordant' to fix the colour, would be boiled and stirred until the required colour came. The women themselves wore plain homespun clothing. A long skirt of dark cloth, often bunched at the back, like a bustle, to make a support for the creels they so often carried, and a blouse, with a shawl or plaid in winter, was their usual attire. They prided themselves on the starched whiteness of the 'mutch', the traditional head–dress which a bride wore on her first morning as a married woman.

The men who, since 1747, had been forbidden to wear their 'habitual form of clothing', with penalty of deportation, mostly wore trousers of 'hodden gray', a woollen shirt and waistcoat. A 'bonnet' kept the head warm, along with the whiskers and beard.

After the repeal of the Act, garments made of 'diced' material could be worn again but the days of coloured 'tartans' did not come till later, when they were worn mostly by the well-to-do and, of course, by the Highland regiments.

A croft interior in Orkney

Women spinning

Skye crofters planting potatoes

Working with a foot plough, the *cas chrom*

A shieling on the island of Lewis

A woman spinning

Kelp burning in Orkney

Cutting peat

6

A LIVING FROM THE LAND

With the establishment of the crofts and the greater part of the hill grazing given over to sheep, the people had virtually to surrender their pastoral habits to become part-time agriculturalists. This must have been irksome to most of them, accustomed as they were to the free life of the herdsman. As the reindeer to the Lapp, so the cattle were to the Highlander.

In the autumn the fattened beasts were sold off and the few kept for wintering were housed; in older times this meant in the end part of the human dwelling. Winter feed was only straw and a little meadow hay. The milk cow was given the best food, for she was the mainstay of the household. Even so, she was most often only fit to calve every other year, and perhaps only gave two or three pints of milk a day. Lactation was short so goats' and ewes' milk would help to tide over the dry period. At a time of dire need, in winter, a stirk which was reasonably fit would be bled and the blood mixed with oatmeal to make what are still known as black puddings.

With the introduction of seed-sown turnips and grass, the demands on the crofter's small arable acreage were great. He would keep only a small number of cattle, the number allowed by his 'souming' (allocation) of hill grazing. Landlords, in the early nineteenth century, were busy 'improving' their estates by the planting of trees. Crofters were then forbidden to keep goats as they damaged the trees by stripping bark. Some herds were feral and still roam the wilder uplands, where they are welcome as they graze the rock ledges which are dangerous for sheep. The old breed of Highland sheep were white or dun in colour and had four or six horns. They were much smaller and less hardy than the sheep of modern times, were housed at night in winter, in rough shelters, and often tethered by day. Only a few were kept for their fleece which was spun into fine yarn, used in making the old 'hard' tartan fabric, and for the ewes' milk, which made good cheese. This cheese is still being made today. Like the cows, the sheep had low fertility, usually lambing every other year.

As the numbers which could be kept declined, the crofters had perforce to keep larger numbers of sheep. The people took readily enough to the pastoral activity of shepherding. Being well used to co-operative effort, they enjoyed the gatherings for shearing, for smearing with a mixture of tar and butter to get rid of maggots, and for tagging and so on. The wool of the introduced black–faced sheep was coarser than that of the old Highland breed and was mostly used in the manufacture of blankets. In 1817 a wool market was established in Inverness for the sale of fleece. As time went by the grazings became soured by over-use. Disease became prevalent and wool was being produced in the emerging colonies. Some of the shine came off sheep-farming on the outlandish scale practised by the landlords.

With the lowland flockmasters had come the border collies, whose descendants work the sheep so magnificently today. For intelligence and stamina they must have no equal in the world. With the shepherds also came the fox-hunters with their brave little terriers, which became known as 'cairns', since they often had to hunt the foxes out of rocky lairs. Dogs had always figured largely in the lives of the Highland people. The great shaggy deer-hounds were legendary, their exploits recorded in poem and story. They were as essential to the way of life of the hunter as the collie is to the shepherd today. Tomchoin, a place in the uplands of Loch Ness country, is said to be the meeting place of the dogs, who were reputed to have the power of speech. Anaconeran, in Glen Moriston, is the place where hounds were bred.

The other working animal of the croft was, of course, the horse. He, too, is recorded in legend, when the 'Elf-queen' carried Thomas-the-Rhymer away to Fairyland on her milk-white steed and he companioned that great horseman, St Michael. The traditional breed of Highland working horse is the Garron. He is small, hardy and very sure-footed, existing on scant feed, browsing happily on hill and moor. The many stretches of rough ground known as 'Caiplich'—the place of the horses—shows that these sturdy beasts were kept in quite large numbers. They were ideally suited to work on croft land, where the fields were small and the implements to be pulled were not heavy. They carried loads of peat from the moor and seaweed from the shore. On the island of Eriskay a special breed of pony evolved, smaller than the Garron but just as useful as a beast of burden. A few of this breed remain and it is hoped they will survive. The Garron, too, is sadly disappearing.

Poultry were kept on the crofts, as with the old native sheep, in fairly small numbers, round the doors with comfortable winter quarters roosting on the roof-beams in the house. Broody hens were treasured as the guardians of future supplies of chicken. The 'loan' of a broody was always welcome! In Orkney, small recesses were built into the walls of the kitchen, where geese could nest in comfort. Like all the livestock, hens and geese had to do a lot of foraging for themselves, and were all the healthier for it. 'Free-range', we call it today.

Bees were kept in small straw 'skeps'. Their honey was prized but the bees themselves did not, as a rule, survive the winter, being replaced by the capture of a swarm later in the year. Boys would be adept at discovering the stores of wild bees in the hollow trees.

The thin, acid soil of the Highlands does not lend itself easily to cultivation. The people always knew they had hungry land and every means was used to feed it. As we have seen, old roof thatch, impregnated with soot from the peat fire, was ploughed into the fields or spread as top dressing. Dung was carted from the byre or the midden and seaweed from the shore. Human excrement was also used. The stalled beasts were bedded in bracken and this, rotted and soaked in urine, was of great value in building up humus. Oats and bere had been grown for centuries. The oats were of the small, black variety, short-stalked, which stood up well to the wind and the rain. Bere was an early form of barley. The meal made from both was used in baking on the griddle and in a variety of dishes and drinks. Bere meal is found in Orkney today, also bere bannocks. Failure of the oat crop meant disaster.

By the time the crofts were set up potatoes had become an important part of people's diet. When first introduced they were considered a somewhat poor green crop. Only later did it turn out that the tubers were the edible parts. Potatoes took up less room than cereals and gave a good return on quite poor ground. It was people's increasing dependence on them which made the crop failures of the 1840s lead to a state of near famine. Still today the potato is of prime importance in the diet of people all over the Highlands. The different varieties are knowingly compared, 'earlies' or 'lates' are grown according to the ground. The crop is stored for the winter in a frost-proof pit and opened during a mild spell for the extraction of what is needed. A dinner without a 'tattie' or two is almost unthinkable!

In the west and on the Islands it was common practice to grow corn and potatoes in 'lazy-beds' or 'finneagan'. These were a development of the old 'run-rig' system. They were long, narrow, raised beds, made by turning two layers of turf, one on top of the other, with a filling of seaweed between them. The raising meant good drainage of the plot. They were fashioned with the foot-plough, the 'cas-chrom'. This was a piece of naturally-curved wood, about five feet long, with an iron-tipped projection and a peg where the foot was pressed, as the worker, moving backwards, turned the clod. It was reckoned that a man, working from January to April, when conditions allowed, could turn five acres of ground.

The foot-plough was used in the cultivation of small fields, where there was hardly any room for the horse to turn, as well as in the making of lazy-beds. Indeed, after the loss of the hill grazing for horses, many crofters resorted to the use of the 'cas chrom'. In Shetland, after the reorganisation of settlements into very small units, the ground would be turned by a 'delving team'. Using short straight spades, they worked in line, abreast. This practice continued into modern times.

For breaking clods and lifting potatoes the 'croman', an implement somewhat like a pick was used. Once the ground was turned, it had to be harrowed, to make a fine tilth. This was done on the lazy-beds with a wooden-toothed implement, like a rake. The oldest field-harrows were made entirely of wood, frame and teeth, and were so light that they were often pulled by women. In the Islands the harrows were sometimes fastened to the horses' tails. This was a barbarous custom but was said to be a good way to break in a young horse.

Harvesting of cereals was originally done with the sickle, which meant that a fairly long stubble was left, as the effort of bending was extremely tiring. Harvesting was a communal activity, though Wordsworth came upon a solitary Highland lass and 'o'er the sickle bending'. By the early 1900s, the scythe had replaced the sickle. Five years later the horse-drawn reaper and the 'binder' came into use on the bigger crofts, hired from the Board of Agriculture.

There were many rites associated with the gathering-in of corn, most of them originating in the pre-Christian times. The first sheaf cut was called the Maiden. It was ornamented and put aside to be given to the horse setting out to plough the following spring. The last sheaf was known as the Old Woman, 'cailleach'. Everyone tried to avoid having to cut it as it was considered to be unlucky. In some places, however, it was built into the top of the last stack, and was thought to provide protection. Late harvests often meant damp grain, and it would have to be dried in kilns. The remains of small kilns can be seen on many crofts today. In Caithness and Orkney quite large kilns were built on to the end of the barn, where they could also serve as an extra room for guests.

After reaping, the crop was threshed and winnowed. In early crofting times the flail, a stout stick attached to another as handle, was used for threshing. The men would work in unison in the airy threshing barns and many a broken nose resulted from a mis-directed flail! Winnowing, to rid the grain of husks, was done either on a piece of high ground or in the draught between the barn doors. The grain was tossed up, so that the moving air could blow the chaff away. Later, mechanical fanners came into use on bigger crofts.

Graddaning, an extremely wasteful harvest practice, had been largely abandoned during the eighteenth century. It consisted of pulling up the crop by the roots, burning off the husk and beating off the grain. It was said that, in this way, the corn could be 'winnowed, ground and baked within an hour after reaping from the ground'. For grinding the corn the earliest device was the 'knocking stone'—*cnotag*—a large, hollowed stone in which the grain was pounded with a wooden club. This method is still used in African villages today. Another primitive grinding device, said to date from Roman times, yet still in use within living memory in some remote places, was the rotary quern. This consisted of two flat round stones, the upper one with a hole in the middle through which the grain was fed. The smaller holes in the rim of the upper stone held pegs which were gripped by the two operators, usually women, who squatted on the ground and turned the stone. The work could be done by a single operator.

Small horizontal mills, dating from Viking times, were set up on burns or lades channelled off streams. Some can be seen in Shetland today. They were in common use until the building of vertical mills in the fifteenth and sixteenth centuries. Some lairds regarded the mills as sources of profit and forbade the use of hand mills, compelling tenants to use the common mill and to hand over a portion of the meal as fee, to undertake the maintenance of the mill and to help transport new mill-stones when they were needed. On some crofts small pedal-operated barn-mills were used for grinding small quantities of grain. They could be easily operated, even by children before or after school hours.

In the eighteenth and nineteenth centuries another kind of mill came into operation in some places—the whin mill. This consisted of larger stones for the crushing of shoots of whin to provide fodder for cattle and horses in the hungry days of spring, when the supply of hay and oats was running out. It was reckoned that an acre of whins could keep six horses for a month. The whins might even be specially sown. They could also be threshed out or bruised on the knocking stone. Today, large areas of whins, no longer used as fodder, brighten the landscape in early spring.

Today, in a time of changing agricultural policies, as the world is being seen as a collection of global villages, there are bound to be changes in the land use. A few years ago that staple Highland crop—oats—diminished. Now the value of the product is being rediscovered, with servings of porridge as a fashionable snack in cafes, oats are being grown again.

Oil-seed rape has taken over large areas in the eastern Highlands. The people have always had to contend with the introduction of new crops, some at the whim of improving lairds, some of which they had never heard and which they refused to sow. The potato appeared in the late eighteenth century. After initial doubts, it was finally accepted as a suitable crop, taking up less room than cereals, and became eventually a staple item of diet. When the crops failed, starvation loomed. There are now new ways of looking at what the ground can produce and of catering to current taste and demand.

Shelter-belts of trees, poly-tunnels and conservatories all allow salad crops and fruit to be grown, even out of season. This is produce which is readily acceptable especially when grown organically, and which, with modern methods of transport, can reach the market rapidly.

7

THE SEA AS A PROVIDER

Families from the great inland glens and straths on the mainland who found themselves evicted to a few windswept acres by a rocky shore must have had an incredibly hard time adjusting to this alien environment. The women learnt to make reasonably palatable dishes of shell-fish and seaweed. The iodine content was undoubtedly healthy. The seaweed, of course, was of inestimable value in making the small patches of land fertile and the small wage earned from working in the kelp industry, while it lasted, would have helped to buy necessities. But lives were lost as men were put out to sea to fish in ramshackle boats, or were swept from the rocks by wind and wave.

In the west and in the Islands, where people never had been far from the sea and where many were of the Viking stock, they were reluctant to depend on the sea as a provider. It had been their highway when there were few roads, and some places were only accessible by boat. But sallies were made in suitable conditions and to be storm-bound was a common occurance. They kept a healthy respect for this unpredictable element—the waters of the sea.

Neil Gunn, the writer whose forbears had been evicted from a fertile glen in Caithness and forced to live on the coast, says in his book *The Silver Darlings*: 'It was out of that very sea that hope was now coming to them. The people would yet live, the people themselves, for no landlord owns the sea and what the people caught there would be their own.'

They had been accustomed to catching fish at the head of a sea-loch by the simple device of a wall built across the shallows, behind which the fish were trapped as the tide receded and could easily be taken in nets. Freshwater fish from loch and burn had always been available, though after the development of the sporting estates they had to be caught by surreptitious means. Even small boys could 'guddle' a trout from the burn. Men would use the 'otter', a line trawled along the shallows of a hill loch, and quickly hide when the look-out signalled the approach of a keeper or ground-officer.

As the fishing industry developed, with the building of docks and harbours, and the provision of sturdier boats, many men, with their seafaring skills enhanced, took work on vessels sailing the seven seas, coming home with some welcome cash and trophies still to be seen in many island homes. They would see to the ploughing before setting off. The women would manage the livestock and the harvesting, as they had long been in the habit of doing. When the herring-fishing was at its height families were well fed, herring in oatmeal providing an almost perfect item of diet. So the sea gave life, though, sadly, it also took lives, often of the young and strong, as the headstones in the Island graveyards testify.

In his book, *Croft Remote*, Tom McIvor describes the local herring-fishing in Achiltibuie, near Ullapool, in the early twentieth century.

In early autumn the shoals would come into Loch Broom to feed on the plankton, their presence noted by the activity of gulls on the same quest. Men would go out in small boats with drift-nets. Two barrels of fish per family was the usual allocation. There was no over-fishing. The fish were gutted and put in brine (salt water), and the barrel left in the barn for several days. The brine was then poured off, the fish re-packed in another barrel, and sprinkled layer by layer with salt. Small bundles of a dozen or so fish were taken to homes with no men fishing.

The nets would then be repaired and water-proofed by dipping into a liquid known as 'cutch', made from the bark of trees. This substance was also applied to the sails, giving them their dark brown colour. After treatment the nets were dried and rolled up.

The summer shoals of saithe, lythe and rock-cod could be caught with a line from the rocks, though this was sometimes a dangerous practice. There were also plenty of haddock, whiting and plaice before the big trawlers plundered sea-lochs and inshore waters.

Gulls' eggs also provided a good source of nourishment. Here again care was taken to see that the nests were not left bare.

8

THE PEAT

To feed the family and the animals on which it depended was the aim of all the year's work—the ploughing, sowing, reaping, herding. To provide another source of energy—winter warmth—another activity was, and in some places still is, engaged in—the cutting of peat for fuel. Wood was scarce in some parts of the crofting areas. Peat was plentiful in most places and the right to cut it was an essential part of crofting tenure.

The work fitted well into the pattern of the year's husbandry. It was a communal activity and was enjoyed as a chance for scattered neighbours to meet, to exchange news and gossip. Sometime in May, when the fields were worked, the crops sown and the cattle out on the new grass, the people would set off to the peat-banks on the hill. The old 'peat-roads', some of which could take a pony and a cart, are still to be seen leading from the settlements. With another winter survived, the larks singing and the air blowing sweet off the moor, there was a feel of holiday about the outing. Baskets of food would be loaded, along with the peat-knives, into the creels or panniers.

The work was hard. The elderly or infirm had their winter fuel won for them by the young and the strong. First, the bank was prepared with the flaughter-spade, 'cabar lar'.

This implement had a long, curved shaft, a cross-bar at the top and an iron blade which was pushed along the ground, skimming off the surface growth of turf and weeds. Then, with the peat-knife, or peat-spade, a straight-shafted implement with flanged blade, the soft peat was cut out in blocks. Working in pairs, one man cut the blocks, his partner, standing opposite, took them up and passed each to the women or youngsters who set them up in small stacks of three or four, to dry.

After a morning's labour the company would relax over a meal of bannocks and cheese, perhaps potatoes baked in the ashes of the fire of heather roots, where the tea-kettle had been bubbling since early in the day. The children, with energy to spare, would scamper happily about, school forgotten, pelting each other with lumps of peat and laughing out of blackened faces!

After a week or two a smaller excursion would be made to the hill, when the small stooks of peat, if dry enough, were piled into larger heaps. In late summer or autumn, perhaps after the harvest, depending on the season, they were barrowed, carted or carried in creels and built into stacks near the houses. In some places the stacks are so beautifully fashioned, shaped so that the water will run off, they could be considered works of art. Indeed, it was once suggested they merit an entry as a Tate Gallery exhibit! In Caithness and Lewis the peat-stacks would often dwarf the dwellings. Peat was such an essential commodity that, in some of the Islands, where there was none to be had on the rock-strewn ground, the people would cut it on another, perhaps uninhabited island, and bring it home by the boatload. Lately, the exploitation of the peat by commercial companies, using

mechanical methods of extraction, has devastated this vulnerable resource. Garden centres have also sold large quantities to their customers. These activities have now thankfully been done away with.

The quality of peat varies from region to region. The brown fibrous kind makes poorer burning than the black, dense type. When thoroughly dry and hard, good peat gives a fine, glowing heat. The warm embers would be covered over with ash at night and blown into life in the morning with the bellows always kept handy by the hearth. In some houses, in older times, the fire was never allowed to go out, even in two hundred years. The only exception to this was when, in a time of extreme disaster or distress, every fire in a community was extinguished and a fresh one kindled by the rubbing together of two rough sticks. This happened rarely. It was known as the 'need' fire, and was lit as proof of the renewal of life.

Today, with heat and light obtainable almost everywhere by electric power, peat is no longer cut on the scale of older times. In fact, its use as a soil-improver in gardens is no longer tolerated.

The cutting by hand was always less harmful than the mechanical method. Crofters, always anxious not to overdo the consumption of any good thing, would treat the 'peatbanks' with care, replacing turves, so that, in time, they would recover. With no heavy machinery involved the ground did not suffer upheaval. Ponies and barrows respect the earth they move on.

Electric power grows ever more expensive. Will power obtained by the action of water, wind, wave and sun eventually be less costly when the man-made installations have recovered their cost?

A fire on the hearth, with heart-warming images in the glowing peat and the scent of the open hill rising from the chimney, these are things which make for wholesome living. They can't be switched on or off.

9

SPECIAL SKILLS

Many Highland women acquired special skills handed on to them, after a long process of trial and error, by their forebears. These skills were in the uses of natural resources as food and as healing agents. These inherited skills are being revived today and made more widely known as people tire of processed foods and medicines with their often unpleasant side-effects.

Oatmeal was the basis of the diet over the years, along with dairy products—milk, butter and cheese. It is said that people thrive best on food which grows naturally in the part of the world in which they live. So the Gaels do seem to owe their health and strength largely to the consumption of oatmeal. The 'sporran', in its original form, was simply a bag made of calf or goat skin, for carrying a supply of oatmeal for use on hunting trips or in a battle. Taken in the morning as 'brose', that is, raw oatmeal, stirred with hot water, salt, milk, honey if desired and even, on occasion, a dash of whisky, was a great provider of energy for the day's work. And, of course, it made porridge and bannocks for the evening meal. The smell of bannocks toasting in front of a peat fire would bring many a wanderer home.

Many a student, too, far from home, survived on his bag of oatmeal. 'Meal Monday' was a day set aside for students to fetch a fresh bag from home. It survives as a holiday in universities today.

Such was the value of oatmeal that it was often used as payment for work done. A most delicious dessert, one which was served to Prince Charlie, is 'cranachan', made with toasted oatmeal, wild raspberries and thick cream, served by many restaurants today.

Of course, the oat crop could fail, the cow could be dry before calving and goats were banned by the improving lairds as they destroyed trees. The women had long been accustomed to looking closely at their environment in the search for supplementary sources of nourishment. Every plant was investigated to see how its various parts—root, stem, leaf, bud, flower—could be used to provide food. Oatmeal was of such vital importance a substitute had to be found and it was. The root of silverweed was dried, crushed, and used to make a floury substance which could be kneaded and made into a kind of bannock. This was not bread as we know it, though the silverweed was known as 'one of the seven breads of the Gael'. The plant flourishes today all over the Western Isles, with its silvery leaves and attractive yellow flower.

The potato took up less ground than the oats and was considered less vulnerable to storm, though in later times it suffered badly from disease. Over-dependence on the potato crop led, as we have seen, to famine in years of blight.

With or without the failure of the basic food crops of oats and potatoes, recourse had always been had to supplementary sources of nutrition. Illness, which could strike at any time, had to be coped with constantly. The summer growths and flowerings were eagerly sought. Heather had so many uses in people's lives, including the making of 'tea' and ale. Robert Burns enjoyed heather tea and Robert Louis Stevenson had a poem on heather ale:

> From the bonny bells of the heather
> They brewed a drink lang syne,
> Was sweeter far than honey,
> Was stronger far than wine.

Heather ale is now found in Highland hostelries!

Sphagnum moss, dried in the sun, was found to be highly absorbent and even antiseptic. It was used to dress wounds during the First World War and it made the first disposable babies' nappies.

Bog myrtle, which grows on the moorland, was used as a deterrent to noxious insects and as a 'strewing herb' to keep away household pests. Today, the oil from the plant is being made, experimentally, into a deterrent to that supernoxious insect—the midge. Myrtle was also, traditionally, a part of the bridal bouquet.

St John's Wort, so-called as it flowers at about the time of the feast of St John, is said to have been used by St Columba, on Iona, to cure a state of melancholy in a young herd boy. Perhaps his lonely job induced depression. The herb was placed in the boy's armpit and he soon recovered his normal spirits. It is known that the plant contains a substance which allows adrenaline to flow, and as the armpit contains nerve-endings, blood vessels and glands, absorption into the system was certainly possible.

Blueberries, growing in patches among the moss and heather, are eaten raw and also made into jelly. Medicinally they are said to help to dissolve kidney stones. Wild raspberries are still the childrens' delight and were prized as medicine for pregnant women, an infusion being made from the leaves.

In damp ground by the roadside grows meadowsweet, or queen of the meadows (spirea). It has long been used for treating fevers and headaches. The great Celtic hero, Cu-Chulainn, is said to have been cured of a fever when bathed in meadowsweet. An infusion of the plant makes a wholesome drink and the flowers produce a sparkling wine.

Even the tiny daisy (day's eye), which opens its petals with the sun and closes them at dusk, has curative properties and was used for disorders of the eyes. The dandelion, in Gaelic lore, was sacred to the goddess Brigid, later Christianised as St Bride. It is a flower to welcome gladly as it emerges in early spring, like a miniature sun. I have read that it is grown commercially in New Jersey. Its uses are certainly many. The leaves are good in salad, the flowers make wine and the roots, dried and ground, make a drink very like coffee.

Chickweed, abhorred by gardeners, was at one time sold at the markets, like watercress. Traditionally it was made into a poultice by bruising a bunch of plants on a hot stone and used to cure abscesses. As an infusion it helps to induce sleep.

The nettle, which grows in abundance near abandoned houses,

is a valuable source of iron and is still put into the broth. The young growth, simmered and thickened with a little oatmeal, with a dash of onion, makes a delicious early summer soup. It is thought that the Romans introduced the plant to Britain as they could not live without it. Its fibres made a fabric. Rubbed on rheumaticky knees it helps to soothe the pain! The sting of the nettle is, as every child knows, relieved by a rub with a neighbouring plant, the docken. In former times the docken root was cleaned, peeled and crushed to make a poultice. Bishopweed (ground elder) was often found near monasteries and inns as it was used in the treatment of gout. Like the nettle, it contains iron.

The leaves of willowherb, that paradise for bees, were often used to make an infusion when tea leaves from India or China were too expensive. The tiny tormentil was used for worming and for dysentery. The tuberous vetch was much prized. Its tubers were dried and chewed like gum, to ward off hunger, a useful attribute when times were hard. The leaves of coltsfoot could be dried and smoked in clay pipes when tobacco was expensive. Thyme made a very acceptable infusion and was also used in a 'nosegay' to stifle noxious smells. 'It imparted courage and strength through' its bracing fragrance, virtues, essential to kings and princes in olden times'. Comfrey, the bone-setter, was spread on splints to help in the healing of bones.

People living on the coasts, particularly on the Islands, and those forced into coastal areas after being dispossessed of their lands in the glens, found seaweed both nutritious and curative of certain disorders, with its high content of iodine. Dulse could be eaten raw or made into soup; thickened and made into a plaster it was applied to the temples to relieve migraine. Carrageen was gathered and spread for rain and sun to wash and dry it, when it could be stored for use in stews and puddings. It was considered appropriate as a food for invalids and makes a most acceptable dessert for people today. Oatmeal and seaweed are much sought after as health foods in our own day and age.

Autumn is the time of the year when the real abundance of natural foods and remedies is clear, with nuts, fruits and berries in bewildering profusion. Hazel nuts contain more fat, carbohydrates and protein than eggs or cheese. They have always formed part of the autumn feasting and still do. Their shells are found in pre-historic middens. Women would walk miles to the nearest market–place, carrying a basket of nuts for sale.

Brambles (blackberries) were made into jams or jellies to last through the winter. A poultice made from the leaves was used to cure skin troubles, and the root, crushed and infused, was taken to help sufferers from asthma or bronchitis. The juniper, said to be the first plant to emerge in the Highlands after the ice age, has berries which were used as an astringent. The whole plant was considered a cure for dropsy. At one time the berries were exported to Holland for use in the gin trade.

Sloes, the fruit of the blackthorn, must be one of the most beautiful of all the autumn fruits, with their purple bloom, like that of hot-house grapes. They are also the most difficult to gather, well guarded by dagger-like thorns. They were used, within living memory, as a cure for sorethroats and winter coughs. Today they flavour gin!

Rose-hips are a great joy for the eye, shining red in the frost, or even in the first early flakes of snow. A daily teaspoonful of the syrup made from them contains enough vitamin C to ward off most winter ills.

Fungi were not used as food or medicine in older times. Perhaps because of cases of poisoning? They were part of the world of the fairy folk. Today they are relished and plentiful among the birch woods—boletus, chanterelle, puffballs and all.

The berry perhaps most prized by the people of the Highlands was that of the rowan tree. The tree itself was celebrated in song and story. Beside every house a rowan grew, to ward off evil spirits. The berries glow among the russet of the autumn leaves and are targeted by hungry hordes of winter migrant birds—the fieldfares and redwings that fly in from Scandinavia, known as the 'snow birds'. There are always enough for humans to enjoy. A jelly made from rowan berries and crab apples, though somewhat sharp, goes well with game or venison. The same mixture, pulped and sieved, makes a gargle and helps in the scourge of childhood whooping cough. Rowan wine is said to contain the secret of eternal youth!

In the days when Gaelic civilisation flourished under the Lords of the Isles there were learned physicians in the land, men who had studied the old Greek texts and listened to sages from other lands. The most famous were members of the MacBeth family from Islay. Their name was subsequently changed to Beaton or Bethune. Their medical learning was forgotten in the general stifling of Gaelic culture which took place in the seventeenth and eighteenth centuries. Today, it is being studied again. In 1878, in Edinburgh, a small group of Highland medical students at the University established the 'Caledonian Medical Society', to promote the study of Gaelic folk medicine. The Society went on to publish the *Caledonian Medical Journal* which contains papers on Highland folk memories of healing.

In our health-conscious age, more and more people are having recourse to the healing and nutritional properties of wild plants, fruits, nuts, fungi and seaweeds. In those crofting areas where organic methods have long been, and in many cases still are practiced, these things can be safely consumed.

Other properties of natural growth are being re-discovered. For instance, in Orkney, the nettle is being gathered and the fibre making a fabric of silky texture. An evening gown of nettles on the market, perhaps?

10

DROVING

Cattle, in the Highlands, had always been looked on as wealth, wealth in a real sense, as sustainers of life, providing meat, milk, clothing, artefacts. Status depended on the number of cattle a man owned. Until about the mid-sixteenth century it was expected of a young clan chief that he would make a raid on his neighbour's cattle. He knew quite well, of course, that the neighbour would retaliate. This raiding was an aristocratic pursuit said to date back to an ancient Indo-European custom. One of the most famous Irish legends concerns the stealing of a bull. *The Cattle Raid of Cooley* is a great prose saga. To take a 'spreidh' of cattle was a proof of the young chief's manhood. Members of some more settled clans would keep watch in the glens through which raiders would pass, posting armed look-outs at strategic points. When a 'spreidh' passed through lands belonging to another clan, a share of the booty was demanded. Failure to pay this could, and did, lead to battle.

The small tenantry, who paid their dues in goods and services, had always depended on surplus stock to provide a small income. When they became crofters their main grievance was that the amount of ground allocated to them was not enough to keep the cattle on which they had always depended.

In the late seventeenth century, when the industrial revolution in the south led people crowding into cities to work in factories and living off bought foods, markets were set up for the buying and selling of cattle. A money economy was taking over. In the Highlands, markets known as 'trysts' were established at Muir of Ord near Inverness, at Crieff in Perthshire, and as far south as Falkirk. Crofters with beasts to sell would join a drive to the markets; they became known as drovers.

The 'trysts' were busy places. There were dealers, with a critical eye for a good beast, auctioneers, pedlars shouting their wares, beggars and entertainers, jugglers and singers. Mostly, the speech was Gaelic, with some English or Scots. The drovers enjoyed their days at the 'trysts', exchanging news and gossip to take back home. The respite was welcome after the hazards of the journey.

Droves might be up to three hundred beasts, with a drover to every fifty or sixty. They covered about twelve miles a day, most of the men on foot, a few riding ponies. Cattle were scared of crossing bridges, preferring to cross water by ford. In the event of a problem, when deep water meant a bridge crossing was inevitable, a drover would take a dozen or so beasts ahead, and the others would follow. Cattle coming from Skye would be swum over the narrows at Kylerhea, swimming nose to tail and dodging the whirlpools. Those coming from the north would also face a swim at Bona, at the east of Loch Ness. At Kyle of Lochalsh they were sometimes loaded into boats. The road-making which was going on at this time meant that the cattle were often shod, like horses, with metal plates, for the latter part of the journey. Blacksmiths plied their trade at various points. Place-names still tell where the 'smiddies' were. The drovers were careful not to press the cattle hard. Some men, still alive in the early nineteenth century, remembered droving days: 'They [the cattle], were in full bloom and full of flesh and hair. If you sweated them the hair dropped down and never got up again into the same condition. The great secret was to take them there as good-looking as they were when they left home. One would think there was nothing but drive and force them on with a stick, but that wasn't allowed at all. They'd go quite nicely when they were left alone'.

After an early start a halt was made at mid-day, at familiar resting-places, when cattle would graze and get a drink. The drovers mostly walked barefoot. As a Skye bard put it:

> Often they did go to Falkirk
> Driving cattle through the mountains,
> And no shoe went on their feet
> Until they returned to the mist which they had left behind.

They carried food—oatmeal with onions, cheese and bannocks, with a 'ram's horn' of whisky. Often they would have to eat the oatmeal mixed with cold water, when a fire could not be made. Occasionally they would be obliged to resort to bleeding a beast, mixing the oatmeal with the warm blood. They slept on the ground, wrapped in their plaids, waking early to shake off the dew or the frost. One or two would watch the cattle overnight, taking the job in turns. Certain well-known stopping places, such as the green at Drumnadrochit on Loch Ness, where drovers from the west rested their cattle, became known as stances. There was no charge for the overnight accommodation as the manuring was valued. In later times, when road-tolls were imposed, some payment had to be made. Occasionally drovers would stop with a shepherd or game-keeper known to them. They seldom stayed at an inn, though Dorothy Wordsworth, writing in her journal in 1803, found Kingshouse, on the moor on Rannoch, 'filled with seven or eight travellers, probably drovers, sitting in a complete circle round a large peat fire in the middle of the floor, each with a mess of porridge in a wooden vessel on his knee'.

The drovers were exempt from the Disarming Acts of 1716 and 1746 and could carry a gun, a sword and a pistol. This was essential as their work was hazardous. Cattle, particularly in the smaller herds, could be carried off by raiders and the drovers attacked. On their return journey they were also at risk, when it was known that they would be carrying money. Sometimes they turned the cash into silver buttons which could be sold later. The dogs would be sent home on their own if their masters were staying on to work. Instinct would tell the beasts where they could find food, as they had on the way down, at a friendly house or farm.

There were bards who took to the droving, bards who found the long days in the hills and glens a time for composition. Rob Donn, the Sutherland poet, often went to the trysts. Some drovers would take home-made goods, wooden dishes or horn spoons to sell. Some would knit stockings as they walked, carve spirtles or quaichs at rest-times. Rob Roy was a drover in his day. Always with an eye on a good deal, he worked a system of 'blackmail', a kind of insurance against the loss of cattle. There could certainly be losses though accident, disease, delays on the way, as well as through theft. Eventually, Rob Roy reverted to cattle-raiding and became a well-known outlaw.

Perhaps the most famous drover of all time was John Cameron of Corrychoille, from Kilmonivaig in Lochaber, who lived from 1780 to 1856. Being adept at the trade, he prospered and came to own several farms and many thousands of sheep and cattle. Joseph Mitchell, the engineer working in the Highlands at that time, describes him thus: 'He was a badly–dressed little man, about five foot six inches in height, of thin make, with a sharp, hooked nose and lynx eyes. A man of great energy, he frequently rode night and day on a wiry pony from Falkirk to Muir of Ord, 120 miles, carrying for himself some bread and cheese in his pocket and giving his pony now and again a bottle of porter... he did not die a rich man.'

Many of the old drove roads are marked on the maps as such and can be happily walked today. Some have been signposted as 'pathways', with distances to the nearest settlement indicated. Some form the basis of modern tarred minor roads. They all lead into the most beautiful areas of the Highlands, through deep glens and over high moorland.

11

THE RITES OF LIFE

For every phase of life the people, in older times, had due ceremonials, with accompanying prayers, poems, blessings and hymns. Pale shadows of most of these ceremonials have survived to this day.

First—baptism was very important. As soon as the child was born, the woman attending the mother would put nine little wavelets of water on the child, singing:

> The little wavelet for thy form,
> The little wavelet for thy voice,
> The little wavelet for thy sweet speech,
> The little wavelet for thy means,
> The little wavelet for thy generosity,
> The little wavelet for thine appetite,
> The little wavelet for thy wealth,
> The little wavelet for life,
> The little wavelet for thy health.
> Nine waves of grace to thee,
> The waves of the Physician of thy salvation.

Should the child die unbaptized, the little body could not be buried with Christian rites in consecrated ground. It would be taken to some inaccessible place, often among rocks. The healthy child would be baptized by a cleric eight days after birth. This baptism was a social occasion, when the child would be passed round the gathering of friends and neighbours, from hand to hand, going sunwise, each person expressing a wish, in verse, for its welfare. This custom, in a simplified form, prevails in many churches today. The child's cradle was traditionally made of sacred wood—elder, rowan, oak—with some iron nails and some objects which rattled to keep away the evil sprits. There was always the fear that a healthy baby would be spirited away and a changeling substituted. Sometimes a rival tribe would be the culprit.

When a son of the house, or daughter, chose to leave home to work elsewhere, perhaps at fishing or on a big farm, the mother would temper her sadness at the parting by singing a blessing:

Mother's Parting Blessing

The keeping of God upon thee in every pass,
The shielding of Christ upon thee in every path,
The bathing of spirit upon thee in every stream,
In every land and sea thou goest.

The next stage in a young man's life was the searching for a bride. A custom still well remembered today was the 'reiteach', or betrothal. The young man would go, with a friend, to the home of the girl he wished to marry, to put his proposal to her father, the girl not being present. His virtues would, naturally be recited by his friend. After a lengthy spell of talk, over a dram or two, the father would acknowledge he had no objection to the bethrothal, as long as his daughter had none. She was then summoned and, if she agreed, she and her suitor would share a dram from the same glass.

A strange custom known as 'bundling' was practised in some parts of the country. The young people, before marriage, would share a bed, fully–clothed, spending the night talking of their hopes, plans, fears, getting to know each other!

It was best to marry on a waxing moon, and not in January or May. Friday, called after Freya, Norse goddess of love, was considered a lucky day for a wedding. The Norse mythology persisted! The wedding would be a great affair, saved up for by several families. On the morning of the church ceremony a white flag, usually a sheet or tablecloth, would be flown from the chimney of the bride's house. The company would walk in procession to the church, pipes playing, guns firing. Guests would gather from far and wide. In the evening there would be a meal in the barn. Chickens, eggs, potatoes, bannocks, butter, cheese, foodstuffs of all kinds, and drink would be brought in by neighbours. After the meal the makeshift tables would be taken away and the floor cleared for dancing. The 'wicked little fiddle' would come into its own, along with the accordion. There would be much teasing and many pranks played on the young couple. Most often the festivities went on for several days or until supplies ran out or the company began to suffer from exhaustion.

Thereafter life began in earnest, with the newlyweds receiving gifts to help them set up on their own—a bag of seed-oats, a load of dung, a coop of chickens, a kist, some chairs. In some places another way of marrying was followed, at the 'handfast stone'. This was an upright stone, in some quiet spot, perhaps in woodland, a stone with holes capable of holding the hands of the betrothed couple. With one witness present they clasped hands, exchanged vows and were considered married for a year and a day. At the end of that time their union could be officially blessed or they could decide to separate. This was certainly a practical state of affairs, even presaging the customs of today! Through the years the couple's lives would move with the small ceremonials of morning and evening.

In the Islands there were often sudden deaths of young fishermen by drowning. Mostly, however, people lived out at least their three score years and ten. Then death might be a release from pain or affliction. As always, neighbours would gather to help. Earth and salt would be placed on the breast of the corpse for the repose of the body and soul. A watch would be kept night and day until the time for interment. The coffin would be carried shoulder-high to the graveyard. If the distance was long, stops would be made at resting-places marked by cairns. These cairns are still to be seen. The 'keening-woman' would walk beside the bier, intoning a lament. The sadness was for the living. For the dead, if one of the faith, the day of death was a happy one.

Bas sona

Day of peace and joy,
The bright day of my death.
May Michael's hand seek me
On the white sunny day of my salvation.

The people always hoped for good weather on a funeral day, so that friends and family could come from afar. They would sing as the coffin was lowered and a piper, a black pennant tied to his pipes, would play a lament. Islands were often used as burial grounds, as they gave protection from depredations from wolves. In graveyards, during the nineteenth century, 'watch–houses' were built where armed men could scare away the body snatchers who sold corpses to medical centres.

After the funeral everyone would be welcomed in the bereaved family's home, where the women and their neighbours would have prepared a meal. Many of these customs are still carried on today, though perhaps in slightly different forms. Funerals are great occasions.

A woman widowed late in life would be visited and looked after. Long before the invention of the Welfare State, no one was allowed to go without a share of whatever the community could provide—food, fuel, shelter.

Birth was often not easy, death was often harsh, the time between had its hazards and its times of joy, but the rites accompanying all the phases of life helped to keep things in some sort of perspective.

12

TIME FOR MAGIC

To the Celtic people, and their descendants the crofters, the notion of the 'other world' was very real. This 'other world' was with them, in the here and now of their everyday life. It could perhaps be sensed more readily by some than by others. People living lives which were sometimes solitary and always in close contact with natural forces had finely honed powers of perception. People, animals, hill, loch, tree, plant, bird, everything observed with the 'seeing' eye could be measured, their movements foretold. Happenings could also be foreseen by those who had the strange faculty of 'second sight'. The Gaelic word for second sight is *da shealladh* meaning 'two sights'—one being a vision of the world of the senses, the other a vision of another world.

In this vision of another world the seer most often was compelled to observe unfortunate events—sudden illness, battle, death. In some cases the precise location of a funeral, the procession of mourners, the carrying of the coffin, would be seen. Those having the faculty of the second sight mostly regarded it as an affliction rather than a gift. It was prevalent in the Highlands and Islands and was commented on by all the eighteenth and nineteenth century travellers in the area.

The most famous of the Highland seers was Kenneth Mackenzie, who lived in the seventeenth century. He was burned to death at the stake after uttering prophecies distasteful to the family of Seaforth, prophecies which eventually came true.

One of his remarkable visions predicted that 'the jaw-bone of the big sheep will put the plough into the rafters and no man will drive cattle through Kintail. After that another day is coming when the sheep will be gone. Strange merchants will take away the land of the great clan chiefs and the mountains will become one wide deer forest. The whole country will be utterly desolate and the people forced to take shelter in faraway islands not yet known. Then will come the time of the horrid Black Rains. They will kill the deer and wither the grasses. Weep for the wilderness of the Gael. After that, long after, the people will return and take the possession of the land of their ancestors.'

These were remarkable prophecies. The predictions regarding the coming of the big sheep, the formation of the deer forests and the eviction of the people to 'faraway islands' have undoubtedly been fulfilled. The 'Black Rains' could well be radioactive fall-out and is perhaps yet to come.

Another faculty attributed to the eye was the power of casting evil spells on people, animals and even substances such as milk. The power of the evil eye was much dreaded. Was it a manifestation of envy on the part of one who sought to inflict harm on someone who, perhaps, was more fortunate than him or herself? Was it a hypnotic power? Was it a question of 'bad vibrations'? Even now in the Highlands, there is a reluctance to accept praise for the beauty of a child or for the beauty of a beast, lest the praise be proof of envy and so a casting of evil. 'The eye of the envious will split the stone' is an old saying.

Evil spells inflicted on animals—the cow or the horse—were especially feared as these animals were the mainstay of life. Even the cow's milk could be drained away and only a useless liquid left.

There were charms for counteracting the evil spells. In a crofting area only some ten miles from Inverness a tale is told of a man who walked fifty miles to Speyside, in silence, to consult someone who had the power to cast out evil. A woman in this same place, not long dead, had spell-lifting powers inherited from her parents and grandparents. Before sunrise she would collect water from a burn which flows under a bridge leading to an ancient graveyard—the

'Bridge of the Living and the Dead'. Into a pail she would put her gold wedding-ring and a silver coin, then pour in the water, mentioning the person's name and adding a blessing—'In the name of the Father, the Son and the Holy Spirit I bless you and may all evil depart from you.' This is a Christianised version of a pagan ritual which survived the centuries.

There were many oral charms to counter the effects of the evil eye:

> It is mine own eye,
> It is the eye of God,
> It is the eye of God's son,
> Which shall repel this,
> Which shall combat this.

Magic lingers in the hearts and minds of many Highland people. A rowan tree grows beside every house as a protection against evil spirits. The wood is never burnt as fuel, even in the coldest winter. A kelpie, that fantastic water-horse, lives in many a Highland loch ready to plunge anyone who rides him into the darkest depths. Many an old woman, loneliness having perhaps turned her into an eccentric, was, in older times, dubbed a witch. Her inherited powers of healing, though accepted, were not understood.

Tir nan Og, the Land of the Youth, that timeless land where youth and beauty lived for ever, was the Gaelic people's idea of heaven, surely a forerunner of the Christian version. Early burials of chiefs contained grave-goods—a sword, a beaker—to ensure a safe and happy arrival in that lovely land. For people living close to the earth, in a harsh climate, with long dark nights and endless summer 'dims', this home-grown magic came naturally to them, as a way of interpreting the meaning of their existence. One wonders whether science, today, is helping them any further along the road to 'knowledge'.

13

RELIGION

To those whose lives depend directly on the forces of nature, on sun and moon, storm, frost, flood and drought, what is known as a religious outlook comes naturally. They have only to observe and to wonder, then worship, tinged with a desire to placate, follows. A rainbow, a comet, an eclipse of the sun or the moon, the stars in their countless millions, these magnificent manifestations contrasted strangely with the harsh reality of existence as they knew it. There was need to find some sort of meaning for life, something which could be grasped, even tentatively, by mind and heart.

The Druids, those wise men of the early years of our era, are said to have foretold the coming of Christ. A leader who dispensed healing, blood sacrifice, death on a tree, these were concepts which could be accepted by the people of the time. The early missionaries of the Celtic church, arriving in the sixth century, wisely grafted their teachings on forms already existing. Water, that essential force, had long been venerated for its power of inward and outward cleansing. Venerated wells were given the names of Christian saints—St Ninian or St Columba. The goddess Brigid became Bride.

In these early Christian times, each simple act of everyday life had an appropriate blessing or prayer. Alexander Carmichael, an Excise officer from Lismore who travelled in the Highlands and the Islands during the nineteenth century, gathered a huge collection of poems, prayers, blessings and incantations. These, along with his notes on the ways of life of the people, have been published in six volumes entitled *Carmina Gadelica*.

He was told, by Ann Macdonald, a crofter's daughter in Lochaber: 'Old people in the Isles sing a short hymn before a prayer. They generally retire to a closet (a small room) or an outhouse, to the lee of a knoll, or the shelter of a dell, that they may not be seen or heard of men. I have known men and women of eighty, ninety, a hundred years of age continue the practice of their lives in going from one to two miles to the seashore to join their voices with the voicing of the waves and their praises with the praises of the ceaseless sea.'

For the start of the day there was the 'kindling blessing':

> I will kindle my fire this morning
> In presence of the holy angels of heaven.
> In presence of Ariel of the loveliest form.
> In presence of Uriel of the myriad charms.
> Without malice, without jealousy, without envy,
> Without fear, without terror of anyone under the sun,
> But the holy son of God to shield me.

For evening, there was the 'smooring blessing':

> I will smoor the hearth
> As Brigid, the foster-mother, would smoor.
> The foster-mother's holy name
> Be on the hearth, be on the herd,
> Be on the household all.

For each daytime activity there was a blessing—a milking blessing, a journey blessing, blessings for the herding, weaving, waulking the cloth.

> Bless, O God, my little cow,
> Bless, O God, my desire.
> Bless then my partnership,
> And the milking of my hands, O God.

Most of the items in Carmichael's wonderful collection came from people of the old faith, the Catholicism of the early Celtic

Crofters gathering seaweed

Modern method of gathering seaweed

A travelling family

A successful deer hunt

An evicted family

A modern croft

Drumbuie

church, before it was taken over by the Roman form. Faith is the
key word. There was faith in the granting of protection against all
forms of adversity, especially illness.

A 'Charm of Protection' asks for:

> Charm against arrow,
> Charm against sword,
> Charm against spears,
> Charms against bruising and against drowning.

There were charms against all forms of physical affliction—
cancer, chest infections, cataract, broken limbs. No doubt the
strength of the faith helped, in many cases, in the healing. That
pre-Christian feeling, still present among the people, mingling with
the Christian, is clear in some of the poems.

Sun

> The eye of the great God
> The eye of the God of glory,
> The eye of the king of hosts,
> The eye of the king of the living,
> Pouring among us
> At each time and season,
> Pouring upon us
> Gently and generously,
> Glory to thee
> Thou glorious sun.
> Glory to thee, thou sun,
> Face of the God of life.

Likewise, the moon was revered:

The New Moon

> She of my love is the new moon,
> The king of all creatures blessing her,
> Be mine a good purpose,
> Towards each creature of creation.
> Be her guardian on land,
> With all beset ones,

> Be her guardian on the sea,
> With all distressed ones.

As a heavenly body, the moon was as important to the people as the sun. Crops were always sown in a waxing moon. As 'Paddy's Lantern', she guided many a lost traveller or seaman home.

Omens were numerous. Most were simply the result of closely observed happenings. Shadows on the loch foretold rain. Certain numbers, certain days of the week had a special significance.

The Day of Saint Columba

> Thursday of Columba benign,
> Day to send sheep on prosperity,
> Day to send cow on calf,
> Day to put the web in the warp.
>
> Day to put coracle in the brine,
> Day to place the staff to the flag,
> Day to bear, day to die,
> Day to hunt the heights.
>
> Day to put horses in harness,
> Day to send herds to the pasture,
> Day to make prayer efficacious,
> Day of my beloved, the Thursday,
> Day of my beloved, the Thursday.

Carmichael transcribed all the items in Gaelic, then set about translating them into English. He was fully aware of the difficulty of his task and often admitted that he could not do justice to the originals. His travels often took him to out-of-the way places. Many times he was cold, wet, hungry, sometimes benighted, but always sure of a welcome by the fireside, with friendly faces, in a tiny house, when he reached the journey's end. The value of his work is, quite simply, incalculable. A whole world comes to life in the hopes, fears, joys of a vanished people expressed in the poems. Most of them were sung, some were intoned in a low voice. In his later years Carmichael continued his work on the mainland, further east. Here he was distressed to find that the things that kept life going—song, poetry, music, dance—were being frowned upon by the leaders of religion. Many people burnt their poems and smashed their fiddles. This was a resurgence of measures against art forms introduced at the time of the Reformation in the sixteenth century.

In 1843 many ministers of the Church of Scotland had led their congregation out—often literally marching out of the building— in protest at the custom of patronage, by which the ministers were appointed at the whim of the local landlord. They formed the Free Church, declaring themselves to be upholders of the people's rights to choose their ministers. Those remaining in the former church mostly sided with the landlords.

Free Church services were held in any vacant building—a mill or a barn—often outdoors, with a portable shelter for the minister and the Bible. The minister lost his home and his salary, but survived with the help of the people.

At the time of the Clearances, the crofters valued highly the support of the Free Church ministers in their struggle for survival. They would walk miles to the Sunday gatherings, to hear the sermon. The sermon, often of great length, was the important element of the service and was delivered in impeccable Gaelic.

This was an invaluable means of keeping the language alive at the highest level. And it helped in the renewal of the people's sense of identity. The singing of the psalms, with a Precentor giving out the first line and the people's voices rising and falling in that inimitable way, which must have come from the old plainsong of the early Celtic church, was next in importance to the sermon.

Until well into the twentieth century Sabbatarianism was strictly the order of the day. The sabbath was a time apart. On Saturday evening water was brought from the well, fuel from the peat-stack, the potatoes were washed and peeled, boots were cleaned. On Sunday, after the church attendance, which might take the whole day if the meeting place was far off, only reading was allowed or an afternoon walk.

In the late eighteenth century Evangelists made their way into many places, setting up marquees, holding meetings and visiting homes. This was partly a crusade against the evils of drink. People did not become teetotal to any great extent. After the passing of the Crofters' Act in 1886, with security in their holdings, they felt a renewal in the controlling of their lives. No measures imposed from outwith could curb the people's spirit. Mairi Macpherson from Skye, Mairi Mhor nan Oran, Big Mary of the Songs, put heart into the people and stirred them into action against the oppression of the landlords. There was a resurgence in the composing of songs and poems.

Religion, from a sense of wonder and awe, through praise and prayer and with a recognition of forgiveness and grace, has been a reality in people's lives which few will deny, though the forms are not always practised.

14

TREE LORE

To the Celtic people trees had a spiritual significance as well as many practical uses. They were considered guardians of great wisdom. The people saw the life of trees, mixed species growing together, their roots firmly in the earth, trunks growing straight and strong, reaching towards the sky, the light, the sun, as mirroring their own. The characters of their symbolic script, known as Ogham, are based on the names of trees. The wonder was that that tiny seed, the acorn for instance, could grow into the massive structure of the oak. The oak inspired the druids to worship. It was associated with strength, virility and so kingship. With the pine and the alder it assumed masculine identity, while the rowan, the hawthorn and the holly were associated with women. The Lords of the Isles carried peeled willow rods, known as the 'rods of justice', on state occasions.

The huge stands of conifers seen about the country now, commercial plantings, are dank, dark places, hardly conductive to the flourishing of wildlife, plant life or insect life. Mixed woodlands of hardy, native trees, growing naturally spaced, offer habitats for so many species.

Over the last few years, in many parts of the Highlands, communities recognising the value of the chance for biodiversity offered by natural forests, are seeking to take over commercial plantings, fell the intrusive elements and replant with native species.

This would allow feeding and space for the red squirrel, the pine marten, the badger and so many other small creatures, butterflies, insect and plant life of every kind.

It is not long since our Highland forebears were utterly dependent on the variety of trees growing round about them. Their house beams were of oak or pine, hazel rods supporting the thatch. Furnishings were fashioned from birch or alder, creels from willow. There was fuel for the fire. Hazel nuts were a prime source of protein. The gean (wild cherry), the blackthorn, the hawthorn and the elder provided fruit for cordials and medicine. The holly, along with the blackthorn and the hawthorn, made a barrier for crops against marauding animals. The life-sustaining qualities of all the trees made them invaluable to the way of life of the time. And the people knew how to sustain their value, with coppicing and pruning, planned extraction and the protection of natural regeneration.

A grove of oaks can play host to a wide variety of life-forms. Lichens grow readily on the trees, providing sustenance for many kinds of insects, which in turn make food for birds and small mammals. Mice, badgers and squirrels thrive on the acorns, as, in older times, did the wild boar. Domestic pigs were sometimes let loose among the oaks. Oak bark was a valued source of tannin, used in the manufacture of leather goods. Twigs were used for brushing the teeth, the tannin keeping them healthy. Oak made the stoutest ships, the natural shape of the trees lending itself to the form required. It was used in the iron-smelting furnaces at Bonawe and elsewhere. The Beltane fires were of oak, kindled with birch.

Another deep-rooted tree, the ash, grows tall and straight and was known in Norse mythology as 'The World Tree', a link between earth and heaven. Spears and chariot wheels were made of ash, as well as ploughs. John Lightfoot, a botanist who travelled through the Highlands and Islands in 1772, published his *Flora Scotica* in 1778. He made a detailed study of many native plants and trees and said he saw a nurse 'put the end of a green stick of ash into the fire and, while it is burning, receives into a spoon the sap or juice which oozes out at the other end and administers this as the first spoonful of liquors to the new-born babe'. Ash was a valued source of fuel as it would burn green or mature. The seed pods, called 'keys', were eaten by people and animals.

The Scots pine was considered the warrior of the tree world. It made the planking of boats, and many trees were floated down the Spey to the shipyards at Speymouth. The rosin was valued as a healing ointment and to make tar. It could be used in oil lamps and reed-lights. Over felling for industrial purposes and to make grazing-lands for sheep has led to drastic reductions in the number of Scots pine. It is slow growing and young saplings are often eaten by the ever increasing number of red deer, but reserves now provide protection for it.

The birch is the most numerous of our native trees. It has been with us, prolific and widespread, for at least 9000 years. It can survive almost anywhere, even on mountain ridges at 2000 feet, and harbours many forms of life. Edible fungi grow in its vicinity, as do mosses, ferns and lichens. Look out for chanterelle in a birch wood. It is the beauty of the forest with its graceful form, its silver trunk, the fresh green of its leaves in spring, the rich maroon of its winter branches. There is no wonder it was worshipped as a symbol of love and fertility. Its practical uses were many. Birch wood made bobbins for the cotton mills in England. Birch bark could make light canoe-like vessels and the inner part served as a writing pad. As Lightfoot says: 'The pliant twigs are well known to answer the purposes of cleanliness and correction.' Birch brooms and the schoolmaster's rod of iron? The sap is extracted to make a very palatable wine. The wood is ideal for the making of furniture, flooring and so on. It was exploited during the Napoleonic wars for the making of charcoal used in the manufacture of explosives. Happily, it regenerates easily and quickly, and today is being protected as its many qualities are being recognised.

The hazel, like the birch, is a hardy tree which flourished even in the semi-tundra conditions after the ice age. It was sacred to the Druids, who used a hazel rod as a 'staff of divination'. Latterly, it was the dowser's preferred rod. To the Celts it represented wisdom. In Celtic lore, nine hazels growing about a pool shed their nuts into the water where they were eaten by the salmon, which became the 'salmon of wisdom'. Hazel nuts are certainly a prime source of nutrition, containing protein, fat and carbohydrates. The wood had many practical uses, making wattling, hurdles, crooks, sticks and shinty sticks. The green shoots, twisted into 'withies', made ropes and harnesses.

The willow is another tree with a long history, going back some thousands of years. The native types are mainly sallow and osier and were highly prized in wicker-making. Lobster-pots, beehives, creels and baskets of all kinds were made from willow. The tree had health-giving properties, too, the catkins being used as lint for dressing wounds and the chemical 'salicin', which it contained, making an early form of aspirin. The value of this substance is being recognised today. Bees get an early feed of nectar from the willow. Deserted lovers 'wear the green willows' to see them through their sad days. Over-coppicing and changes in land use may be threatening the willow yet a new tree can so easily be made by pushing a stem into the ground. It shoots up in no time at all. Let us hope this magical tree may not be allowed to disappear.

The rowan, of course, is the most magical tree of all. One grew by every house, protecting it and its inhabitants from harm. A branch was placed over the door to the byre, ensuring the safety of the cattle. It can grow at great heights in the smallest pocket in the soil, between the rocks. As we have seen, the wine made from its berries is said to contain the secret of eternal youth! From the time of the Druids its place is safe in the land of legend and myth.

The alder is an ancient tree which likes to grow in wetland and in forests. In older times these alder forests made safe refuge for runaways or outcasts. Diarmid and Grainne, the eloping lovers, took refuge in the alder woods of Argyll. The timber, which had resistance to water, was used for making mill wheels, milk pails and bridges. Furniture makers prized it for its deep red colour which gave it the name 'Scotch mahogany'. The green wood made whistles and pipes of exceptionally sweet sound. Alder leaves in boots relieved tired or aching feet. Today, a huge alder may be seen at the Mound in Sutherland, a manmade wetland. There is also a smaller one at the Govert, near Drumnadrochit.

Many smaller trees flourished in the native woodlands. The gean and the bird cherry are welcome for the beauty of their blossom in early summer and for their fruit, sour for humans but favoured by many birds. They are found also in remote spots, in high and lonely glens; a delight for the traveller. They were not exploited, though bowls and other small items were made from their attractive wood. The elder, like the rowan, is often found near dwellings and was reckoned to have magical, protective powers. The smell of its leaves does deter many insects, but in early summer its creamy white flowers have a pleasant scent and can be made into a sparkling wine. Its berries, too, have many uses, medicinal as well as nutritional. One celebrated physician would always doff his hat when passing an elder tree, so highly did he regard its properties. Elderflower water, for eye and skin lotions, can be found in chemist's shops today. The travelling people made spoons and forks from the wood, and the stems, which were easily hollowed, made pipes for musical instruments. Sadly, the elder does seem to be disappearing, as craftsmen's skills are dying, cheap wines are imported and customs as ancient as man are being forgotten.

The hawthorn, the 'May tree', with its white blossom, which must never be taken into the house, is linked to otherworldly hallowed things of the wild. In former times rituals were carried out in groves of hawthorn. Its early leaves were eaten as a fresh green bite and were said to be helpful in the treatment of blood pressure. From their taste they were known as 'bread and cheese'.

The blackthorn was considered a malignant little tree on account of its vicious thorns, its twisted shape and the bitter taste of its fruit, the sloe. Today, this is added to gin to make the well known sloe-gin. The berries also have medicinal value and at one time were thought to be a cure for the dreaded epilepsy. It is not always realised that the blackthorn is the original plum tree of today. It is invaluable as impenetrable hedging and can still be seen planted along boundary walls. The wood was traditionally used to make clubs—the Irish shillelagh—shinty sticks and walking sticks, the crooked stick of the Highlander, as Harry Lauder knew!

The juniper is one of the first trees to have emerged after the end of the ice age, some 10,000 years or so ago. Twigs were considered a cure for the curse of the 'evil eye' and were carried by seamen as protection against drowning. The branches made a smokeless fire which was of great help to the illicit distillers of the nineteenth century. A burning branch was carried through the house at Halloween to oust the evil spirits lurking there, and also the hidden germs. During the nineteenth century there was a lively export trade from Inverness to Holland of juniper berries for use in the making of gin. The juniper is beginning to disappear but there are calls for it to be saved.

These are only a few of the native trees which have flourished in the conditions of soil and climate of the Highlands and have been invaluable in the lives of the people. At various times attempts at reafforestation have been made, after the over exploitation of the trees. The plantings being undertaken in various parts today are mixed and self sustaining; leaf-litter and dead debris providing nourishment for the roots, and the four layers—the lowest of mosses, fungi and lichens, the next of flowers, the next of shrubs and the top canopy of leaves—providing habitats for wildlife of every kind.

With coppicing and the appropriate management of woodlands, the old woodmen's skills in making hurdles, now used as garden fencing, and charcoal for barbecues are being revived. Crafts still known and practised are the fashioning of hazel wands into walking sticks and willow into baskets of many kinds. The woods are coming alive.

In Abriachan, an upland area to the north of the Great Glen, the local community has taken over a large acreage of woodland previously planted by the Forest Commission. It is felling the intrusive conifers and re-planting native trees. A 'Stewardship Accreditation' has been received for this environmentally friendly project. There has been some clear fell and some thinning to let in light. Sawn branches are sold as firewood or sent to a nearby factory for conversion into chipboard.

The native trees planted include Scots pine, birch, aspen, willow, gean (wild cherry), bird-cherry, rowan, holly, oak (a few), hazel, ash. Seed is collected from trees in the area.

One man working a croft has got part-time employment as a driver, transporting felled trees to the roadside. Another works part-time as an administrator. A local man is Forest Officer and there is seasonal work for several others. It is interesting to note that the original Gaelic alphabet corresponds in the initials of the names of trees. Thus:

Ailm (elm), Beite (birch), Coll (hazel), Dur (oak), Eagh (aspen), Fern (alder), Gath (ivy), Huath (white thorn), Iogh (yew), Luis (rowan), Muin (vine), Nuin (ash), Oir (spindle-tree), peith (pine), Ruis (elder), Suie (willow), Terne (furze), Ur (heath).

15

THE CEILIDH

Whatever the season had held—drought or flood, storm or long days of calm when the evenings grew dark and chilled by the autumn frosts—people would meet for a ceilidh. A sigh for a failed crop or a gleam in the eye at the thought of glossy beasts, it made no difference; to be alive and together was good.

Usually one particular house was a favoured one as a meeting place and so was known as a ceilidh house. Neighbours would gather as darkness fell, each one bringing a small contribution to the evening's enjoyment—milk or bannock, cheese or peats. The women would often work hard at their knitting or spinning, the men at carving or mending an implement. The children would stay quiet in whatever corner they could find as they waited, with suppressed excitement, for whatever the ceilidh would bring.

When the company was complete, tobacco exchanged for a pipe-fill, the comments would come—on the weather, the doings of the laird, the ongoings in the outside world. Then the *Fear an Tigh*, the man of the house, would need little urging to tell a story. With their prodigious memories the people could repeat the tales of long ages ago, handed down by their forebears. Particularly popular were the old epic tales of Finn MacCoul and the Feinne, the soldiers of fortune who became an order of chivalry in the third and fourth centuries and whose exploits took them all over

Ireland, to Scotland and into Europe. Tales of Deirdre and her lover were especially popular with the women. Sometimes the stories would continue over several evenings before the end was reached.

Alexander Smith, in his book *A Summer in Skye*, published in 1865, wrote: 'In the stories which are told round the island peat-fires it is abundantly apparent that the Celt has not yet subdued nature... In these stories and songs man is not at home in the world. Nature is too strong for him, she rebukes and crushes him. And this curious relation between man and nature grows out of the climatic conditions and the forms of Hebridean life... Gathering wildfowl he hangs like a spider on its thread over a precipice on which the sea is beating a hundred feet beneath. In his crazy boat he adventures into whirlpool and foam. He is among the hills when the snow comes down, making everything unfamiliar and stifling the strayed wanderer. This death is ever near him and that consciousness turns everything into omen.'

When the man of the house had told his part, leaving everyone anxious for more, he would call for a poem or a song from the company. The poems came readily, for poetry was the natural form of expression for a people steeped in myth and legend, and as close observers of their surroundings, of hill and moor, sea, river, and loch, their powers of description were innate. Closely linked to poetry, of course, was music. Most poems were meant to be sung. At the end of each verse the singer, with a movement of the hand, invites the company to join the chorus. Anne Grant of Laggan, in her *Letters from the Mountains*, said of Speyside in the nineteenth century, 'In every cottage there is a musician and in every hamlet there is a poet'. This could be said of many parts of the Highlands and Islands.

When clan society flourished the chief had a bard among his followers. The bard was a highly skilled, professional poet who recorded events, acted as historian and genealogist and commented on people and affairs in polished verse. He also praised the chief and could incite the clan to warfare. The bardic training was rigorous. Aspiring students were lodged for months in a remote place and had to lie for long hours in a darkened room, with a heavy stone on their chests, memorising and composing poems. In this way they learnt to recite many hundreds of lines and verse. It is said that Saint Columba attended one of these bardic schools in Ireland and composed twenty 'Lays'. Satire was a feature of many compositions and was used as a weapon against unpopular people. This satire was greatly feared and could even result in the death of a person cruelly satirised.

After the decline of chieftainship the bardic tradition was carried on by 'township bards', working crofters who had no bardic training but who had the innate skills needed for composition. Sadly, because this composing was all in the oral tradition, much of it has perished. Writing was not encouraged, from early times, as it was thought to harm the memory. However, thanks to the nineteenth century collectors—Alexander Carmichael and also J.F.Campbell, Margaret Fay Shaw, Frances Tolmie, Father Allan Macdonald of Eriskay and others—a good store has been put down in writing and faithfully translated.

At the ceilidh, when the company had worked up a thirst with singing, there would be tea and bannocks and a dram or two. If there was a fiddler itching to play, the young and some of the elders would be up on their feet. Movement was a grand way to express joy or shake off sorrow. In the old style of step-dancing with its quick, intricate foot work, all the space needed was the size of the top of a wooden gate post! This form of dance was exported to Nova Scotia with the emigrants, who maintained the tradition and are now bringing it back home. In the late nineteenth century, when the fiddle was deemed 'wicked', the accordion, commonly known as the 'box', was adopted as a suitable accompaniment to the dance and has remained so.

As the people settled down again, loath to part company, there would be a request for riddles, a form of entertainment known through the ages, even, it is said, back to the time of the Queen of Sheba, who propounded riddles to Solomon.

Thus:

> A little clear house
> And its two doors shut. (an egg)

Four came over
Without boat or ship,
One yellow one white,
One brown, abounding in twigs,
One to handle the flail
And one to strip the trees.   (the seasons)

If the riddle was not solved the propounder went home as the 'King of Riddles'. Proverbs and sayings were also very much appreciated.

Night is a good herdsman; she brings all creatures home.

When you get up see that the grass rises with you.

St Columba's robe will not fit every man.

The three most beautiful things in the world—
a full-rigged ship, a woman with child and a full moon.

After a reluctant leave-taking, neighbours would grope their way home in the dark, perhaps with a glowing peat for a torch, and cries of 'haste ye back' from the host family.

Today, the word 'ceilidh' is most often applied to what is more a concert-type entertainment, in a hall with people appearing on a stage to sing or play an instrument. The music may be Highland, but the spontaneity and the fun of the small gathering is lost.

16

WORK SONG

Song is in the very nature of the people of the Highlands. It comes as naturally to them as everyday speech. It is thought that some of the first tunes were based on the piping of the redshank on the shore. The words come from close observation of the world around them, of the hills, the sea, the creatures, their fellow beings and the events they were all involved in.

There were the bards, of course, as we have seen, those semi-official poets who composed verse for singing, mostly praise-poems in honour of chiefs or incantations to incite clansmen to battle. The people, working on the land and the sea to sustain their families, found words, airs and rhythms springing naturally into their lively minds, and voices to help them through the hours of hard work which their living demanded.

There were songs for every kind of activity. Those for communal tasks—reaping, rowing, waulking (shrinking) the cloth—had a strongly marked rhythm to suit the synchronised effort of the workers. For the more solitary occupations of the women— churning, spinning, weaving, working the quern or handmill— less emphatic rhythms were needed, though they were timed to fit the movements involved. For milking, many a soothing song was sung to persuade that sometimes capricious creature, the cow, to give generously of her milk.

The length of time needed to accomplish a task was often

reckoned in songs: 'We'll need twelve songs to finish the field' the men might say, as they set off to work. A band of men, reaping with the sickle, would need a song that brought a story to their attention. Sometimes, to pass the time, they would sing a boasting or taunting song, known as 'flyting'. If this meant a quicker cutting of the crop it might, also, lead to a certain amount of danger from sharp sickles if the taunting went too far.

The 'iorram', or rowing song, had, of necessity, a strictly regular rhythm to keep the rowers in time. It's thought that the well-known song 'Over the Sea to Skye' has a verse-metre of the 'iorram' type and could well be sung by rowers today:

> Loud the winds howl, loud the waves roar,
> Thunderclouds rend the air,
> Baffled, our foes stand by the shore,
> Follow they will not dare.

A rowing song from Ness, in the island of Lewis, goes like this:

> *Verse*: Row thou, dear Kenneth
> *Refrain*: Neil, son, 's na ho ro.
> *Verse*: Love of young women, maidens' darling!
> *Refrain*: Neil, son, 's na ho, ro.
> Ho, ro, ho, ro.

All songs for communal activities consisted of a verse, sung by a leader, and a chorus in which all joined. The refrain most often contained nonsense syllables which just helped the tune along. The verse often told a story, perhaps taken from a long poem such as 'The Galley of Clanranald':

> Let our spring be not awkward,
> But without languor or failing,
> To trust yourselves to the sea-grey tempest.

This 'iorram' contained fifteen verses, each to be sung twice. In the rhythm one can visualise the pull of the oar in the water and the pushing back, ready for the next stroke. The astonishing feats of memory of illiterate people mean that the words of many of these songs have been handed down though generations and are sung today, though the methods of working have changed.

The reaping and rowing songs were the earliest to go out of use, though the early eighteenth century travellers to the islands, Johnson and Boswell in particular, noted them. Many were taken into the repertoire of the most common labour songs, those sung at the waulking (shrinking) of the newly woven cloth. The task was carried out by a group of women sitting round a long board, sometimes a door taken down for the occasion. The cloth, which had been soaking in a tub, most often of urine, was laid on the board, gripped by the women and passed sunwise round, with a hearty thump. This was something like an African drum beat and made for excitement among the workers as they sang in voices of deep timbre. The leading woman would sing the verses, often of a satirical poem poking fun at men, for the waulking was strictly a woman's province. All would join heartily in the refrain, the thumping and the accents of the music coinciding. Sometimes an extra beat would add pith to performance. As the cloth got drier and lighter the tempo increased, rising almost to a frenzy. Occasionally one of the women would come up with an impromptu verse recording some recent event. No song could be repeated for fear of bad luck.

In very old times the 'waulking' was done with the feet, the women sitting on the ground and making kicking movements. This must have been less conducive to the singing of the songs, even satirical ones! Though the shrinking is now done, of course, by mechanical means, women still sometimes sing the old waulking songs for pleasure, holding a piece of cloth as they sit round the room and moving it to the rhythm of the music.

For the solitary tasks which the women undertook there were much quieter songs. Spinning songs kept time to the spin of the wheel and the beat of the treadle. Spinning could be pleasant work, done outside the door in good summer weather.

The milking songs were very important, milk and its derivatives, butter, cheese, buttermilk drinks, being an essential part of the diet. The songs expressed affection and praise for the precious house-cow, who had a name and was looked on as almost one of the family, sharing the dwelling in older times. Each cow had her best-loved song. Alexander Carmichael quotes a milking song of several verses:

Lovely black cow, pride of the shieling,
First cow of the byre, choice mother of the calves,
Wisps of straw round the cows of the townland,
A shackle of milk on my heifer beloved,
Ho my heifer, ho my gentle heifer.

For churning, watching the milk turning into butter, almost incantatory verses were composed:

Come, thou churn, come
Come, thou churn, come,
The churning made of Mary
In the fastness of the glen,
To decrease her milk,
To increase her butter,
Buttermilk to wrist,
Butter to elbow,
Come, thou churn, come,
Come, thou churn, come.

Working the quern, moving those heavily grinding stones, was an onerous task for women and a monotonous one. A song was essential to keep the work going. One such is from Barra:

Quern, quern, grind!
Quern, quern, grind!
Old woman, grind the quern
And you shall have the quern bannock.

To quicken the movement the second verse changed:

Quern, quern, grind!
Quern, quern, grind!
Old woman grind the quern
And you shall have the good man's son.
Faster I will grind and feed [the quern],
I will feed and grind!

If singing a child to sleep is considered work, there were certainly many lovely Gaelic lullabies:

The nest over the laverock,

> My little one will sleep and he shall have the bird.
> The nest of the mavis
> Is in the bonnie copse,
> My little one will sleep and he shall have the bird.
> The nest of the curlew
> Is in the bubbling peat-moss,
> My little one will sleep and he shall have the bird.

As well as the work songs there was, of course, music for life in all its phases. 'Puirt a Beul', or mouth-music for dancing, was devised with the banning of pipe and fiddle music during the religious revivalist movements of the late eighteenth and early nineteenth centuries, and very effective it was, and still is! At a time of death there was 'keening', a dirge sung in the house and the 'coronach' sung by a mourning woman in the procession to the graveyard, which extolled the virtues of the deceased and expressed the grief felt at the death. There were also many 'fairy' songs, some telling of relationships between human and fairy folk, some happy, some sad.

Many of the songs—work songs and others—are still sung by Gaelic emigrants overseas, particularly in Cape Breton and many other parts of eastern Canada. Sadly, they are seldom heard in the Islands now, but we are fortunate indeed that far seeing people, over the last one hundred and fifty years, have collected and preserved so many and have managed to record some of the last singers.

The work songs were many, for the everyday tasks were many and singing set a rhythm on labour. There were also songs for the quiet hours— love songs of poignant beauty, songs in praise of the glens or hills, hunting songs of great length to keep the hunters happy. All these were memorised by people with uncluttered minds. Some twentieth century collectors tended to 'tame' these songs, cutting them down into verses, providing accompaniments in Victorian drawing room style or in that of military bands. Today, there is a lively revival of traditional, unaccompanied singing.

At the 'Mod', that annual gathering of Gaelic musicians, where competitiveness tends to prevail, there is now an award in memory of Màiri Mhór, the Skye Poet, whose songs inspired the people during their times of stress. A Mairi Mhor fellowship has also been set up. This allows the holder to teach traditional singing in schools and colleges.

17

ILLICIT DISTILLING

In the late eighteenth century, with the continuing pressure for an increase in monetary rents and the price of the cattle fluctuating, people began to look for a means of obtaining some income. At that time the brewing of ale was dying out in many parts, and as wine from the Continent, in particular claret, was penalized by heavy duties, a trade in whisky looked promising.

In the old *Statistical Account of Scotland*, published in 1796, we read: 'Distilling is almost the only method of converting our victual [barley] into cash for the payment of rent and servants and whisky may, in fact, be called our staple commodity.' Until this time wine and ale, with some rum and brandy smuggled from the west coast, had been the favoured drinks in the Highlands. From early days sap had been extracted from birch trees and allowed to ferment, to form a kind of wine. The botanist Lightfoot, writing in 1777, in his book *Flora Scotica*, says 'Formerly the young tops of the heather are said to have been used to brew a kind of ale, and even now I was informed that the inhabitants of Islay and Jura still continue to brew a very potable liquor by mixing two thirds of the tops of heather to one third of malt.' It is interesting to note that birch sap wine and heather ale are being drunk in the Highlands today.

In 1609 the famous Statutes of Iona had prohibited the import to the Islands of wine and what was known as 'aqua vitae'. Distillation had been going on, on a small scale, in the privacy of people's homes. As soon as the business began to expand, the government, always eager to find sources of revenue, began to impose licenses and impediments. These harsh measures meant that the business of distilling had to go, literally, underground. The work was often carried out in caves or dugouts. It was a skilled affair but it was also a ploy which intrigued the men as a challenge to authority. Harsh measures were imposed to restrict the activity. In the west the military were called in and revenue cutters sailed the coasts. In inland areas riding officers were employed. One of these, in the Lowlands, was Robert Burns who wrote, in a poem written in 1785,

> Tell them wha hae the chief direction,
> Scotland an' me's in great affliction,
> E'er sin' they laid that curst restriction
> On aqua vitae;
> An' rouse them up to strong conviction,
> An' move their pity.

One wonders where his sympathies lay! The restrictions were certainly considered injudicious, vexatious and injurious. They positively encouraged illicit distilling.

One area of the Highlands, in the hills to the north of Loch Ness, was particularly well known for its 'smugglers', as the illicit distillers became known. It was well-sited, difficult to access from the main lines of communication, had an abundance of water sources and of peat for fuel. The people had long been in the habit of making small amounts of 'uisge beatha', the water of life. It was considered an essential element in the fight against the winter ills brought on by cold and damp. It lifted the 'black dog' of gloom which descended on the shoulders in the long dark. And, of course, it gladdened weddings and comforted the bereaved. Who has not savoured a 'hot toddy' on a winter night? The process of marketing the product meant, of course, that many dangers had to be confronted—fines, imprisonment, confiscation of equipment and so on. The liquor had to be carried secretly to inns, hidden in a load of peats or potatoes, in coffins, hearses and even bee-hives.

The officers of Excise would sail up and down Loch Ness,

looking for the tell-tale smoke of bothy fires. But often juniper was used in daytime operations as it is a smokeless fuel. Sometimes the officers would stay overnight in the schoolhouse so as to be quick off the mark, night or day. The 'smugglers' were certainly not going to give up their bounty without a struggle. It was a skilled craft they were engaged in, carried out with improvised equipment, in damp and dark locations. The grain would be steeped in the water of the nearest burn, laid out to germinate in a hidden outhouse, spread every twenty-four hours, then transferred to a peat-fired kiln to dry. Next, the mash was boiled for a couple of hours over a peat fire and the process repeated. When fermentation ceased the distilling took place, the hot vapour from the boiling mash rising through a copper pipe known as the 'worm', where it condensed to a liquid. The 'worm' inevitably became worn. When this happened the men would dismantle the whole outfit, leaving the worn-out worms, then report to the nearest Excise officer the finding of a 'still', claim the £5 reward for information, buy a new 'worm' and set up another still in another place.

Ways of outwitting the Excisemen were many and various. Lookouts were posted everywhere. When the smugglers' were actually tackled in their homes many ingenious devices came into play. A man known as the 'King of the Smugglers' in the area where he lived, once got his wife to show the officer round the outbuildings while he laid his old father on the kitchen table disguised as a corpse, covered with a sheet, with the tell-tale cask well hidden underneath. No officer would dare touch a corpse. Sometimes a grandmother's skirt, plumped up as she sat, warming herself at the fire, would make a secure hiding-place.

On one famous occasion the Excisemen captured a large cask of whisky, taking their prize to the upper room of a nearby inn. There, they took refreshment brought to them by a servant girl. She had been bribed to tell the smugglers the exact position of the cask in the upper floor. They then bored a hole directly beneath and into the cask so that the contents flowed into another below, which they quickly removed. That hole became a feature of the inn for many years!

Stills were hidden in various places, even in a church pulpit after the beadle had been bribed with a large dram. Casks buried in the peat, that great preserver, lay hidden for years. Imprisonment as a punishment for smuggling was not regarded as a disgrace. Prisoners were even allowed home on a Sunday and returned unfailingly to complete the sentence. Some landlords turned a blind eye to the practice of distilling, knowing that at least it assured them of payment of rent.

John Murdoch, an Excise officer who travelled the Highlands and Islands in the nineteenth century, seeing the poverty of the people, took the chance to encourage them to resist the oppression of the landlords. Alexander Carmichael, another Exciseman, recorded his invaluable collection of Gaelic song and story when on his visits to the Islands at that same time. No mention of smuggling appears in his work or in that of other collectors. Nearer our own days, Neil Gunn worked in the Excise department. Doubtless his travels gave him pause for thought when he came to write his great novels.

By 1823, when vigorous measures were being adopted to stamp out smuggling, it is recorded that 4000 people in one area were fined twenty shillings for illicit distilling and four guineas for selling without license. These were large sums of money at the time. Some men caught red-handed in their bothies received prison sentences.

In the later nineteenth century evangelical movements were preaching teetotalism, emigration had been taking place and gradually skills were lost, along with the hidden equipment. But, who knows, in some remote corners of the very glens where the official drink is made today, some secret bothies may yet be producing their quota of tasty drams.

Today, the making of wine for home consumption and also on a commercial basis is practised quite widely. Sap is extracted from the birch, the berries of rowan and elder, the flowers of dandelion and meadowsweet and many, many more, making healthy and attractive drinks.

In Orkney, beer is still made in the traditional way.

18

THE SUMMER WALKERS

Welcome visitors to crofting areas in the summer months were the vagrants, or wanderers. Sometimes a single man on his way from a spell of work, perhaps at the fishing, travelling from the east to his home in the west, taking the well-known track through the hill, would appear among the community. He would be made welcome, get a sleep at the fire, a bowl of brose in the morning and bannocks to see him on his way. It was the old tradition. A stranger was never refused food or shelter. In older times there had been those who took advantage of the custom and left their host impoverished. But the summer walkers who came by in company were independent in their ways, making their shelters of willow wands and tarpaulin and cooking on wayside fires. Their knowledge of the uses of plants as food and medicine made them adept at living off the land. Summer berries, autumn nuts, gulls' eggs, a trout guddled from the burn, a rabbit or game bird snared with skill and cunning, wild honey, herbs of all kinds, all these gave them the abundance enjoyed by the hunter-gatherers of old.

Their coming would be noted from far-off—a small procession of men and women, young and old, some walking, some riding in an old ramshackle cart, pulled by a lean horse, children gallivanting, dogs racing ahead or staying to heel when shouted back. Many of these people were descendants of clansmen who had been 'out' in the '45, had taken to the heather and never returned to settled conditions. They still had pride in their ancestry, many claiming they were 'Royal' Stewarts. Some were skilled craftsmen, perhaps erstwhile smiths, highly regarded members of a community, who had adapted their skills to the making of tin-ware. The goods they produced were of high quality. Some worked in silver, some made horn-spoons.

Many of these travellers had vast stores of traditional tales tucked away in their minds, handed down through the generations and ready for a telling. Still today they can be heard recited orally or on tape, and many have also been transcribed by keen collectors. Music was there too, with a tune scraped from an old fiddle and a song by the evening fire.

The travellers were also, like the wandering bards of past ages, bearers of news from other parts. This made them doubly welcome, in the days before radio and when newspapers were scarce and many could not read. Listeners would greet them heartily when they stopped to unload their burdens, put up their shelters and light their fires, as they prepared for a stay of a week or longer on a patch of wayside grass. If extra hands were needed to get in a crop of oats before the weather broke, if turnips needed singling, if the tatties were ready for lifting or the peats for carting home, walkers could always be called on to help. The reward might not be money, for that was always scarce, but barter came more easily and meant the reality of a goodly portion of butter, milk, eggs or rabbit skins to make winter clothing. This was satisfactory for all concerned.

Other summer visitors were the packmen, who came singly, walking miles along the old tracks and drove roads, carrying their wares on their backs. For people who went rarely to shops or markets, their coming was welcomed, particularly by the women, who caught a glimpse of luxury at the sight of ribbons and lace among the mundane buttons and threads as the pack was opened on the doorstep. The packmen dealt in barter, too, though money was welcome if it could be spared. They carried news, which was as welcome as their wares; news from the town where they bought their stock, news of the wider world, of political intrigue, news of distant friends or relatives at whose houses they had called.

Occasionally, a strange character would arrive, someone clearly schooled in the ways of the world, who had been to many parts but who preferred his own company and that of the hills and forests. Encountered at the right moment, he would delight a listener or two with tales and would share his experiences and his knowledge of the contents of books of many kinds. One such stranger who wandered up the braes of Glen Urquhart, in Inverness–shire, must have inspired many young men to go exploring.

Members of the old wandering families still come about the crofting areas in the summer months, in old cars or trucks now, bringing bought goods, small textiles, knitting wool and so on. Most of them are settled these days in the towns, and no longer have the look of sparse, but healthy living. Some still hanker for the freedom of the road and tour the country, dealing in scrap metal and spare parts. The magic of their coming has gone but we are fortunate, indeed, that we can still hear their stories told.

19

SCHOOLING

It was John Knox, back in the sixteenth century, who advocated 'a school in every parish' and also that girls as well as boys should be taught. It was to be many years before his vision was realised. But learning had always been an important part of Highland people's lives. During the sixth century, in the small monastic settlements of the missionary followers of St Columba, local boys were taught the rudiments of Latin and Greek to enable them to join in the simple forms of Christian worship practised there. They were also trained in the basic skills of husbandry and even metal working. Later, the abbey provided schools, mainly for boys from the more important families.

King James VI, in the famous Statutes of Iona of 1609, used education as a political tool, making it imperative for the sons of all the higher echelons of society to be sent south, to be educated in English, so that he would be provided with a highly competent class of administrators. This was the first of many measures adopted in the 'civilising' of the Highland people.

A hundred years later, in 1709, a group of professional men in Edinburgh, fearful of the rebellious spirit of the Highland chiefs, set about establishing the Scottish Society for the Propagation of Christian Knowledge, which advocated a form of education based on religious principles and the teaching to be in English. There was a certain amount of opposition from the chiefs, some of whom had, though reluctantly, provided premises, mostly woefully inadequate, and teachers for the parish schools.

The Society set up schools in many places in the Highlands, and so began the slow erosion of the native language and its designation as an inferior tongue. One school, in Fort Augustus, was forced to close, as the pupils were making no progress: the English language being unintelligible to them. In 1767 a concession was made by the authorities—some instruction in Gaelic was to be allowed. However, speaking in Gaelic by the children, even in the playground, was strictly forbidden. Severe punishments were inflicted on those caught doing so.

The scholars were each to bring peat to keep the schoolroom fire going. The master had a small salary, supplemented by the proceeds of the annual cock-fight where boys paid a fee to enter their birds and the master got the makings of his Sunday dinner! The hours of attendance were long. From February to October the school was open every weekday from 7am to 11am and 1pm to 5pm. In the depths of winter the hours were 8am to 12pm and 1pm to 3pm or 4pm. Often the children could not venture to school at that time of the year on account of storms or ill-health. Holidays were few, apart from the summer break and a day or two at New Year. Christmas and Easter were barely recognised. The three R's and some history and geography were diligently taught. Some 'lads o' pairts' were given lessons in Latin and in advanced mathematics. Meanwhile, local poets, whose work had hitherto been transmitted orally, took advantage of the education they had received to transcribe their work and make it available for translation into English.

After the establishment of the crofts, many of them in remote places far from any centre of education, the people would often take turns to have a student, on his summer leave, to stay in their house. In return for his board and lodging he would instruct the children in the basic skills of reading, writing and counting.

During the nineteenth century a wider world was opening, a world of cities and strange countries and with this came the realisation that English was the language spoken in these places. A knowledge of English was becoming the passport to prosperity.

Parents, wishing their children to escape the hardships of the life they had known, encouraged them to speak English, even in the home, though they themselves had little or no knowledge of this foreign tongue. Some even got the children to teach them a few words of English so as to make communication easier.

Those who moved away, still always eager to keep in touch with home, had to take to letter-writing. Writing, either in English or in Gaelic, did not come easily to many and most could not afford postage. Unstamped letters could not legitimately be opened but often the handwriting and the postmark were enough to let the would-be recipient know that the sender was alive and, hopefully, well.

Mail was brought by a runner in the more remote places and the schoolmaster would act as a 'receiver of mails'. He would also often undertake to read to the recipients those letters which were stamped, and to write replies on behalf of parents who themselves had perhaps no schooling or had forgotten how to hold a pen. Newspapers would also be sent to the schoolmaster and he would read aloud to an arranged gathering any items of national, or local, importance.

After the passing of the Education Act in 1872, attendance at school for children between the ages of five and thirteen became compulsory. Some parents found it hard to comply with this directive. The children, from a very early age, had been in the habit of helping with work on the croft—herding cattle, gathering sheep, peat-cutting, potato-planting, harvesting and so on. Many a day they could not be spared from these tasks. The long summer break was known as the 'harvest play', almost a contradiction in terms for the children involved! Attendance officers were employed to visit the homes and check on the circumstances. In some cases of prolonged absenteeism from school the parents could be fined.

In the log books kept by headmasters from 1872 onwards many reasons for children not attending school are instanced. For one child 'who lives in a very high and cold place' lack of boots is given as the reason she could not make the journey to school. Also, parents were extremely fearful of infections, perhaps with the memory of the cholera epidemics in the 1840s in mind. They kept their children firmly at home until the school premises had been disinfected by the burning of sulphur and the walls freshly whitewashed. Tuberculosis and diphtheria were deadly scourges much dreaded by the people.

Gradually, however, the schools became centres of welfare. Hot drinks of cocoa were provided, there were visits by a nurse to check on minor disorders and later, vaccination against smallpox was administered. Some landowners, now known as heritors, seeing the way things were going, became members of school boards, providing occasional treats for the children, outings to places of interest and also prizes for achievement.

The appetite for education was strong, particularly as there was the prospect of employment, on a seasonal basis, in the building of the Caledonian Canal between 1803 and 1822, and later, in the construction of the railway, when English speaking was the order of the day. This work allowed the crofter to return home at vital times, such as harvest. The passing of the Crofter's Act in 1886 gave the people an impetus to keep the land and buildings on the croft in good order. In some schools evening classes were arranged for those who had left school early and these were well attended.

In the late eighteenth century the Paisley firm of J & P Coats (manufacturers of thread), in order to promote education, gave school-bags and books, along with glass-fronted bookcases, to many schools so the children could become familiar with the works of Scott, Dickens, Fenimore Cooper and R.M. Ballantyne, improving their English, but with a further loss of their Gaelic.

The young people of the crofts were by now bilingual and would remain so all their lives. Today, many of further generations regret that their parents had, perforce, to make them abandon their native tongue in order to pursue careers in the growing industries or in the professions. That native tongue, known as the 'Language of the Garden of Eden' was, until quite recently, spoken by the Highland emigrants in Nova Scotia. Traditional music, song and dance were also enjoyed there. With the coming of television, traditional forms of communication and enjoyment have almost disappeared now, in the face of American input.

In the early 1960s children from orphanages or from unsuitable homes in Glasgow, Greenock and elsewhere were being placed in crofting families, to be brought up along with their offspring. For this the families were given a small allowance. Mostly the town children grew into sturdy adults, some eventually marrying into their adoptive or neighbouring families. During their upbringing they were well supervised. The 'Cruelty Man', one still remembered in places in the Great Glen, visited the houses regularly. Fostering, of course, had always been a part of Highland life, from the days when the clan chief would place a son of his in the care of a clansman. In those days the bond between foster-father and foster-son and between foster-brothers was very strong. One would willingly die for the other if the occasion demanded.

Today many small Highland schools have been closed, the children transported to bigger places where they can enjoy the benefits of all the technical equipment deemed essential in modern education. In those that stay open, much of value remains. Gaelic is taught, along with French, reading is encouraged, there is story-telling and singing, all on the small, intimate scale that is so precious. The children learn about the history of their area, and go on outings of discovery. They make a garden, plant trees and help in the general life of their surroundings. Two schools in the Highlands, at Elgol in Skye and at Dochgarroch on Loch Ness, have been given eco flags, which they proudly fly, to show that they really care for their environment by protecting wildlife, recycling waste, clearing litter and so on.

They play shinty, a game uncorrupted by commercialism, as well as football. All this ensures they grow up with a sense of belonging, of having an identity, which they can carry with them as a lifelong asset.

20

THE LAND WARS

The visitor to Skye today, enjoying the peace and beauty of the island, would find it hard to visualize the scenes of violence which occurred there in the early 1880s. There were events of the same sort in other crofting areas, but those in Skye were particularly distressing.

With the landlords intent on making their estates pay by the setting-up of large sheep-farms and sporting establishments, a money economy had come into being in the Highlands. The crofter, on the diminutive holding to which he had been banished, on the coast or the barren moor, was now being asked for an increase in his rent. Non-compliance would mean eviction from the house built by his own hands, from the few acres which gave him at least some sort of subsistence.

In 1873 John Murdoch, an Excise officer who travelled the Highlands, founded in Inverness a newspaper—*The Highlander*—in an attempt to make the crofters' grievances known. Articles in English and in Gaelic were published, along with poems. Murdoch believed passionately in the value of the Gaelic language, that it was part of the identity of the people and must survive along with them. He addressed meetings, collected funds and gradually persuaded crofters to protest.

Mairi Macpherson, known as Màiri Mhór on account of her stature, a Skye woman, composed powerful verse which did much to put heart into the people. Her poems were recited at ceilidhs and at public meetings. A passionate advocate of land reform, with a firm conviction that the land belonged to the people, she helped to secure the victory of popular candidates in local elections all over the Highlands. Gladstone's Land Act of 1881 had given security of tenure and judicially determined rents to small farmers in Ireland. Encouraged by this, and by the increasing number of sympathisers to their cause, the people of the Highlands began to stir.

At Martinmas in 1881, the tenants of Braes in Skye marched to Portree to declare their refusal to pay their rents until the grazing for their cattle on Ben Lee on which their livelihood depended, which had been given over to the landlord's sheep, was restored to them. The following April, the Sheriff Officer went to serve eviction orders on a dozen tenants. He was accosted by a crowd of 150 and the summonses were burned. Five crofters were arrested. The situation was so alarming that Sheriff Ivory of Inverness–shire asked for assistance from the Glasgow constabulary in restoring order.

Before dawn on 19 April, a bitterly, cold, wet day, fifty policemen, with Sheriff Ivory in the rear, set off from Portree to march to Braes. Taken by surprise, the people were thrown into confusion. Most of them were away at the fishing, but a crowd, mainly women, managed to rally on the hillside, whence they rushed at the police, stoning them into desperation. Several arrests were made. This encounter became known as the Battle of the Braes. A monument at the roadside now records this significant event. Many journalists were present, with photographers, and the account they sent to their papers, which included the *Illustrated London News*, gave wide publicity to the crofters' cause. The few arrested men were treated sympathetically by the authorities in Inverness, given small fines and came home as heroes. Sheriff Ivory was refused military help, for which he had hoped, but the police force was strengthened by fifty constables.

In the following October a messenger-at-arms, a police-inspector, a superintendent and nine constables were prevented from entering Braes by a crowd which set about them with sticks and stones. In December, the ironic outcome of the struggle was that Ben Lee, which had been part of their holdings, was leased to the crofters for grazing. Meanwhile, the crofters of Glendale, in north-west Skye, were refusing to pay their rents. Four policemen and a messenger-at-arms, who were despatched with summonses, were set upon and beaten up. Thereafter, several hundred crofters, armed with sticks, scythes and graips, marched to Dunvegan to find that the police had fled.

Early in 1883 the government was compelled to take action. In order to avoid military intervention five Glendale crofters were persuaded, and finally agreed, to stand trial in Edinburgh. They were sentenced to two months' imprisonment and became known as the Glendale Martyrs.

Meanwhile, the government was setting up a Royal Commission to inquire into the condition of the crofters and cottars in the Highlands and Islands. Under the chairmanship of Lord Napier, a Lowlander, were Sir Kenneth Mackenzie, Donald Cameron of Lochiel, Charles Fraser Mackintosh M P, Sheriff Officer Nicholson and Professor Mackinnon, all these of Highland origin and several being Gaelic speakers. On 8 May the Commission began taking evidence at Braes. A crofter was defined as 'a small tenant of land with or without a lease, who finds in the cultivation of his holding a material portion of his occupation, earnings and sustenance and who pays the rent directly to the proprietor'.

Most of the crofters chosen to appear before the Commission spoke only Gaelic and had to depend on interpreters to convey the meaning of their statements. Typical of the situation is this encounter of Angus Stewart, a crofter in the Braes, with the members of the Commission, as recorded in the published proceedings. He was asked to state his occupation, where he was born, whether he was freely elected. Then he was told: 'Now you will have the goodness to state to me what are the hardships and grievances of which the people complain who have elected you...' 'Yes, but it is in Gaelic that I prefer to speak. I want the assurance that I shall not be evicted from my holding. I would not have a fire at my house on Whitsunday.'

Angus Mackay from Farr in Sutherland said: 'We and our fathers have been cruelly burnt out of Strathnaver, like wasps, and forced down to the barren shore, where we had in many cases to carry earth on our backs to form a patch of land.' Murdo Maclean, a crofter from Uig in Lewis, said that 'there is one day set apart by the gamekeeper upon which you are allowed to go and pull heather to make ropes to fasten the thatch on the houses... you cannot attend on another day... or you are liable to be fined for it.'

The Commissioners spent many months listening to evidence from crofters in all parts of the Highlands and Islands. Meanwhile, crofters who were at Fraserburgh for the herring fishing began to hold protest meetings and to issue circulars about Land Law Reform. The unrest was still most acute in Skye, where fences were pulled down, ricks fired and sheep driven from grazings. In November 1884, the government sent a gunboat with three hundred marines and a steamer as a mobile police barracks, and an armed force marched from Uig to Staffin. A truly dramatic show of strength! The Commissioners duly published their report, while agitation continued. At last, after much deliberation, in 1886 the 'Crofters' Act' was passed. This gave security of tenure to the crofters in their holdings and compensation for improvements made. It set up a Crofters' Commission to fix fair rents, subject them to review and cancel arrears. It still did not, however, restore to them an adequate amount of land.

The Highlanders, who were traditionally a pastoral people, largely dependent, as we have seen, on the rearing of cattle, could not live with their land turned into sheep farms and forests. Rebellion still flared. A month after the passing of the Act, 750 police and marines were landed on the island of Tiree. Eight crofters were arrested and five were imprisoned. In October, Ivory sent police and marines to serve summonses again on crofters in Glendale. The party was assaulted by the women while the men drove the cattle into the hills. Gradually, the work of the Crofter's Commission began to take effect as the rents were reduced and arrears cancelled.

The demand for land was still acute. At Park, in Lewis, the people raided a deer forest and killed a hundred deer. They made a makeshift camp, using sails as tents, and roasted meat over fires in the open. Some carcases were sent home to hungry families. Troops were sent to quell the unrest and remained in occupation for two years.

As time went by, profit from the large scale sheep farming

enterprises was diminishing as the ground became soured from over-grazing, and competition from the emerging colonies in Australia and New Zealand forced down the price of wool. Consequently the landowners began to further develop the estates as sporting venues. They, themselves, had always enjoyed the pleasures of the chase. Those who could afford to do so could entertain large parties of guests during the shooting season. The glorious 12th of August would see these parties arriving by train at Inverness for their onward journey to the lodges of their hosts. Some of these lodges were in the most remote parts of the estate and the journey was long, by road, sea or on horseback.

People of the south country, at this time, among them wealthy industrialists, were looking for an escape from the crowded cities. Queen Victoria and her husband Albert enthusiastically extolled the pleasures of life in the Highlands of Scotland, which led to an influx of visitors and travellers. More lodges were built and huge expanses of hill ground were let out to sportsmen from the south and from America. This provided employment for some of the tenants, who acted as gamekeepers, ghillies and stalkers. Good stone houses were provided for the keepers. On the more prosperous places employees were made to wear suits of specially designed tweed. Crofters, who were accustomed to planning their own day, were initially reluctant to take work which left them at the beck and call of their employers. Those who became keepers were loathed and feared by their contemporaries for their fierce protection of the game. There were deer and grouse in plenty on the hills, salmon in the rivers and trout in the lochs. The keepers reared pheasants, hand-fed, then released them to the shooters. The crofters could not take even a rabbit for the pot.

Large areas of ground, now known as deer forests, were fenced off with high wire, so depriving crofters of grazing for their cattle. In some places, the deer were allowed to wander indiscriminately, making raids on the crofters' small crops of hay and oats. In spite of protests, no compensation was made for these losses. Many smallholdings in the vicinity of the lodges were taken over to provide produce for the shooting tenants. The people displaced were given ground in remote marginal areas.

One sporting tenant in Glen Urquhart, a Mr Bradley Martin, who had made a fortune on the railways in America, employed a large number of people during his stay. He entertained lavishly. As well as those working on the sporting side, there were indoor jobs for domestic staff of all kinds, cooks and gardeners. The blacksmith was kept busy, as was the coachmen and the wheelwrights. All this activity was, of course, seasonal. Bradley Martin did provide treats for the children and built a village hall which is still in use.

Another American tenant on a nearby estate was renowned for his prowess with the gun and for his way of slaughtering the deer as they were driven towards the shooters en masse. The finesse of stalking was not for him. He is remembered for the huge wire fence that he had built to keep the deer from straying and for his prosecution of a crofter who allowed a pet lamb to graze the wayside grass on the estate.

One page of a typical game book for 1884-85 shows the extent of the depredations of Highland wildlife made on a sporting estate in one year. As well as the usual prey—deer and game birds—it includes one hundred and three ptarmigan, seven capercaillie, fifty plover, two peregrine falcons, twenty-one owls, one hundred and fifty-nine wild cat and seventy squirrels.

Apart from the few who found seasonal employment, crofters in the vicinity of the sporting estates were not much better off than the wildlife. As always in times of fear or sorrow recourse was had through the rallying call of the bards. Poems telling of 'every field and corner under moss since the son of the deer has put us in disarray and banished us to a distant land... the customs of our forebears have undergone a change...' and 'a new song about the destruction of the crofters, the many glens they have made desolate, with the deer in the place of people'. Many of these poems were published in the pages of the *Oban Times*. They were sung at fireside ceilidhs and at public meetings, inspiring the crofters to new insurrections. *Tha moran ri dheanamh fhathast*—'there is still much to do' was the current saying.

In 1892 another Royal Commission was set up to look again into the state of the crofting communities. People appearing before the Board to testify were estate factors, valuers and other agents, some speaking at great and tedious length. Crofters were in a minority.

At the fourteenth sitting of the Commisssion at Drumnadrochit, at the east end of Glen Urquhart, on 4 July 1893, Hugh Macdonald, a blacksmith and crofter, stated 'Gentlemen, in my opinion there is a considerable amount of land in Glen Urquhart suitable for new holdings... and there is also among the people a strong desire for such land. In the deer forest of Balmacaan there are many acres of arable land. Some have been planted. Much arable land has been added to the home farm... there were a number of families... the ruins of some of the houses are still standing and much of the old arable land is still under heather.'

In an addendum to the report of the Royal Commission, the Rev Malcolm MacCallum from Argyll, the member who seemed to have the greatest understanding of the crofting people and their concerns, stated: 'The unanimous report of this Commission and the evidence led before it in my opinion conclusively proves that there is urgent need for the settlement of the land question in the Highlands... with respect to the land cleared for sheep and deer and constituting an area much more extensive, valuable and fertile than that in the occupation of crofters, the landlords have appropriated the clansmen's rights and interests in it without payment of compensation of any kind. The solution of the Highland problem is not land purchase but the resumption of the clansmens' rights to occupy the Fatherland... the demand that the cleared lands, now lying almost wholly waste, should be made available for the enlargement of present holdings is a call for simple justice and more consistent application of the main principles of the Crofters' Act.'

Overgrazing by sheep and deer have, of course, wreaked havoc in many parts of the Highlands: sheep graze close, deer damage or kill saplings. When cattle were the predominant grazing species the ground was healthy, well manured, and the lush weed growth trampled. The bracken which now infests large areas was regularly cut as it was used as bedding for the housed beasts, for thatch and manure. The rushes also were controlled, used as thatch for ricks and so on. The small bright patches of green in the old shieling grounds tell of how the land might be. Sheep numbers were limited to the number allocated to each crofter's 'souming'. Now the numbers are in accordance with the rate of subsidy. Deer are being culled. In many parts they are being farmed. The transcripts of the sittings of both the Royal Commissions can be found in the reference library in Inverness. Reading them brings to life the struggles endured by the crofting communities over the years. Only today is the possibility of real change in the ownership and management of land in the Highlands becoming a reality. It is in the forefront of political thinking and, more importantly, within the grasp of activists on the ground.

To return to the aftermath of the reports of the two Royal Commissions, it was not till ten years after the passing of the Crofters' Act that the government of the time tried to improve conditions for the crofting communities. The Highland Congested Districts Board was established, and funds made available for building roads and bridges, for developing the tweed industry and the fisheries, for fencing and draining and for a stock improvement programme, with the provision of bulls, tups and stallions. These measures were important, yet still the people's craving was for land.

In February 1906, raiders landed on the island of Vatersay, ferried over their sheep and cattle and built houses for their families in the places from which their grandparents had been evicted. Sure enough, ten of the raiders were imprisoned, but eventually the Congested Districts Board managed to buy Vatersay, after a tussle with the owner, and the raiders were given their holdings.

In 1911 the Scottish Land Court was set up. To this Court, appeal could be made in any case of injustice. The newly established Board of Agriculture was given certain powers to settle people on land, the owners receiving compensation.

After the First World War, some attempt was made to help land settlement with orders of compulsory purchase and loans to landholders, but continuing discontent led to further raids taking place. Crofters who had been evicted from the fertile parts of Raasay to the barren rocks of Rona, an islet to the north, returned to reclaim their original holdings. As a result several people were imprisoned.

By the early 1930's emigrations overseas, some of it assisted, and to the towns and cities, with the attraction, for the younger people, of easier living, had reduced the number of those still determined to follow their traditional lifestyle. Those who stayed found that their ways had to fit more and more closely into those of the world at large from which they were no longer isolated. Modern methods of communication of many kinds were developing. With the outbreak of the Second World War, cropping programmes and livestock rearing had to be regulated to fit the needs of the nation at large. Grants and subsidies were forthcoming as a beleagured island looked to its native providers for sustenance. When peace came there was some slackening of effort, but war-time conditions had shown what could be achieved in bringing marginal land into cultivation. To encourage people to stay on the land, perhaps in larger amalgamated units, as living standards had risen, ancillary occupations were more essential than ever. These were now in construction work on roads, and in hydroelectric schemes, in forestry and in tourism, as well as in traditional fishing, hand-loom weaving and so on. These enterprises could provide employment, some of it seasonal, in the crofting areas, thus allowing crofters to maintain their grip on the land and the basic elements of their accustomed lifestyle.

In 1954, Professor Taylor of Aberdeen, who had been asked to form a Commission of Enquiry into crofting conditions, reported: 'The crofting system deserves to be maintained, if only for the reason that it supports a free and independent way of life which, in a civilisation predominantly urban and industrial in character, is worth preserving for its own intrinsic quality.' These were brave and wise words.

Frank Fraser Darling, that forward-looking conservationist, writing in the 1950s, in the chapter on the ecology of land use in his book *The Future of the Highlands*, says 'while the Hebrideans were dependent on the environment for their whole subsistence a very beautiful ecological adaptation to circumstances took place... When a culture is beginning to break down, its disciplines of existence also begin to fail and the empirical conservation of habitat at which the people had arrived breaks down to exploitative attrition of natural resources.' Is this the point we are reaching today?

The following year a new Crofter's Commission was set up to

administer the Crofters' (Scotland) Act 1955. In terms of this Act the Commission must keep under review all matters relating to crofting, see to the re-letting of vacant crofts and the apportionment of common grazings and administer schemes of financial aid such as grants and loans. A statutory register of crofts was to be kept.

Six years later, certain amendments were made to this Act. Flexibility was needed as the pace of change in the world at large was increasing and it was becoming apparent that crofting must be linked to some form of industrial activity of a permanent kind.

The croft and croft house could still form the basis of family life, with the wife, as had always been the case, bearing the burden of day-to-day living, tending cattle, sharing field work with neighbours and so on.

The creation of the Highlands and Islands Development Board in 1966 gave impetus to the idea of industrialisation, as part of the remit of this body was to promote non-agricultural development in the crofting areas and thus to provide employment for the crofter and, importantly, for his family.

Investment in the tourist industry was one way in which, it was hoped, this could be achieved. This is certainly an industry which can be developed right on the doorstep of houses in the more remote communities. Grants and loans were made available for the provision of additional accommodation, catering and other facilities for holiday visitors in the croft houses, in chalets or on campsites. In some instances the whole house would be let for the summer months while the family lodged in a converted outbuilding. Tourists, however, were not always welcome. They often disturbed stock, left gates open or damaged fences. The crofter really enjoyed the privacy of his holding.

In its first report, in 1967, the Board stated: 'Crofting... if one had to look now for a way of life which would keep that number of people in relatively intractable territory, it would be difficult to contrive a better system. But its future depends on other employment support. This the Board accepts as a clear challenge and duty.'

A pulp mill was built near Fort William and an aluminium smelter was established near Alness on the east coast. These enterprises were not as successful as had been hoped. Indeed, they served to empty some of the glens of men who subsequently became unemployed and drifted off elsewhere. Also, they required the input of workers from run-down industrial areas, who required schooling, housing and medical care. This resulted in an overload on the existing facilities. At various times during the eighteenth and nineteenth centuries, attempts had been made by landowners to promote industrial activity in the Highlands, using natural resources. The Sutherlands had developed coal mining at Brora. In Glenstrathfarrar lead and graphite mines were established. In both cases imported labour was needed and in both cases this meant miners from Wales. In some parts the remains of their little houses can be seen. In Glenstrathfarrar, also, and in other places, mills were built for the manufacture of bobbins for use in the cotton trade in the south. These enterprises gave employment to some crofters, but they were short-lived.

In 1991, the Highland Board was replaced by another development agency—The Highlands and Islands Enterprise Network, with its regional agencies in various parts of the area.

In 1993, another Crofter's Act set out to encourage young people to take over crofts and to encourage crofting townships to cooperate in undertaking developments ancillary to crofting agriculture, which would be of common benefit and to improve the quality of livestock. A panel of Assessors maintains communication between crofters and the Crofters Commission. The Commission advises the Secretary of State on crofting matters.

The discovery of oil in the North Sea and the entry of Britain into the European Economic Community, matters of great importance, were closely studied by the Commission and their impact reported on to the government. Many jobs in the oil industry are now compatible with the running of a croft. Workers may be employed in shifts of two weeks at a time on an oil-rig, followed by two weeks' leave, when the croft work can be undertaken. Again, much devolves on the wife and the family at home!

So many Acts and so many agencies have tried to keep crofting communities active and forward-looking. Now, at last, many of them will be able to have their own say in the matters affecting their lives.

Francis Thompson, who was brought up in the Island of Lewis, in his book *Crofting Years*, published in 1984, says 'The future of crofting and of the crofters lies firmly embedded in legislation. Only human will, urged on by the best of motives, will ever prise it out of its statutory stagnation for the benefit of those whose attitude to the land of the Highlands has been proved to be the best in the past. That past could live again.'

He continues: 'Only when the Highlanders and the people of the Islands themselves are in control of their own destinies will the Highlands and Islands begin again to make their unique contribution to the socio-economic fabric of the nation. And only then will there be a regeneration of confidence in native ability to work out their own destiny for themselves.'

21

TODAY

Today, the policy of the government, the Crofter's Commission, Highlands and Islands Enterprise and all bodies connected with the land is to keep people in a working situation in all parts of the Highlands, even the most remote.

Derek Cooper, a man with roots in Skye, who has written much about the islands, says: 'The Highlands have so much that is good, rare, even unique in human experience. If the people there and ... the rest of Scotland realise that there is a choice, that it must be made soon, and decisively, then not only can what is good be saved, but a future built in the Highlands and in the whole of Scotland that could inspire the rest of the world.'

Another writer on the Highlands, James McMillan, in a book *The Anatomy of Scotland* by Leslie Frewin, says: 'The Highlands are Britain's safety valve: a reminder that man does not live by power stations alone: a romantic challenge to the prevailing obsession with economic growth. If the Highlands have to be "privileged" in the accountant's sense of that word, then let them be privileged.' That was written in 1969. Since then many enterprises in all parts of the country have been grant-aided. The Highlands are not unique in this regard.

This is what the Crofter's Commission has to say to the subject: 'The primary objective for providing financial assistance in a crofting context is to support the retention of population and promote active communities.'

Crofting is not merely the working of a small agricultural unit: it is a way of life, a way of living on the land, in small, interactive communities. This implies many things—concern for the well-being of all, respect for the environment, pooling of resources, sharing of labour. This is the way it always was. This is the way it can be today.

The Crofters' Commission is actively engaged in pursuing absentee tenants in crofting communities. On a positive note they have introduced the Croft Entrant Scheme, whereby people between the ages of eighteen and forty, having identified a croft, are entitled to an ingoer's Management Premium; the outgoing tenant receiving an incentive payment. The sums may vary. In some cases the sitting tenant may stay on in the house, the incomer getting a grant to build a new dwelling. The Scheme is administered by the Project Officer of the local Enterprise Company. The entrant is expected to take up residence on the croft and to prepare proposals for its development. Advice is given on the preparation of the development plan. To quote the Croft Entrant Scheme leaflet: 'There is more to crofting than its economy. Culture, environment, heritage are also cornerstones of Crofting.'

Two people who recently came into crofting through the Scheme are Robert Baker and Charlene Macleod (née Cameron).

Robert Baker took over a croft of seventy-three acres in the island of Islay. The outgoing tenant said: 'I am delighted to be able to pass on this croft to a capable person and his young family. Mr Baker has considerable agricultural experience. He has undertaken a programme of fencing and dyking and has, with grant aid, built a fank and a shed. He runs some Aberdeen Angus cattle and black-faced sheep. His hobby is sheepdog breeding and training. His wife grows herbs and makes quilts for sale at the markets.'

Charlene took over her father's croft in Drumbuie, between Kyle and Plockton. After an initial spell of extremely hard work in stone removal, road repairs, drainage and so on, Charlene, with help from family members, has got the croft to produce crops of oats, hay, potatoes and turnips, grown the traditional way, in rotation, on 'run-rigs'. The surplus is sold locally. Charlene has been a catalyst within the community. Elected Township Clerk and Assessor, she focused community spirit and organised an entry to the Township of the Year competition, which resulted in an award of £5000 from Scottish Natural Heritage. Since then many developments have taken place in the community. Charlene now drives the school bus. Her husband, who is a builder, has built a house in an apportionment of the common grazing. Their two children attend the local school.

When the crofts were originally established, some two hundred years ago, they were not meant to provide a complete living. It was intended, as we have seen, that crofters should have additional employment in the fishing or kelp industry or on the estates. Today the Commission is encouraging the development of ancillary employment on the crofts. Small businesses may be established, for instance, in the marketing of produce or of craft work. Where facilities are available, a business can be run by new information technologies, the operator commuting only from the kitchen to the attic, saving much wear and tear.

For well-balanced projects for imaginative use of land, particularly those which might deliver positive benefits to the community as a whole, grants and loans are available, as are Livestock Improvement grants. Advice and guidance on the production of plans for projects and for possible financial aid from other sources is provided.

The Crofting Reform Act of 1976 had given crofters the option of acquiring their land, at a reasonable price, based on the rent paid, but there was not a big uptake of the offer. Many crofters felt adequately assured of their status under the existing Act, as long as the Land Court was there to deal with any problems they might have.

The Commission, always eager to encourage interest in crofting matters, issued an attractive, illustrated pack for use in schools, so that young people could get a glimpse of life on a croft.

In 1992, with the 'Right to Buy' in operation, the community in Assynt acquired 300,000 acres of croft land and established a Trust to manage the area for the good of the community. Since then, much development has taken place. A hydro–electric scheme has been built, loch fishing improved, with re-stocking and boats provided for anglers. Cattle stocks have increased and sheep are fewer, to everyone's approval. There has been some planting, particularly of shelter-belts.

Bill Ritchie, some twenty years ago, was told he would never get anything to grow on those barren, windswept acres in Assynt. Since then, in small hollows, sheltered by birch and hazel, hollows which had received liberal dressings of shell-sand, peat and seaweed by the crofters cleared from the glens, he and his wife have grown crops of the must succulent vegetables, as well as the familiar tatties and roots. They are all, along with herbs of many kinds, organically grown. The surplus is sold to the two hotels in the district. Guests are amazed to find spinach, squash and fresh fruits of many kinds on their plates, all produced locally.

Over the last few years communities in Knoydart and the islands of Eigg and Gigha have managed to buy the land they live on. In Eigg, the former laird's house has been bought by a couple with two young children, who plan to turn it into a centre for 'sustainable living', with courses on environmentally friendly building techniques, solar and wind power, organic gardening and ecology in general. The community is currently working to restructure crofting land in the Cleadale area. So many people have applied for crofts there that conditions have been imposed, to make sure that the most suitable applicants are accepted. In Abriachan, near Inverness, as already mentioned the people bought woodland from the Forestry Commission. They are replacing the plantations of commercial conifers with trees of native origin. They have also developed the recreational side of the enterprise with the making of pathways, a bird hide, a tree house, picnic areas and so on. For the few crofters still working in the area there are part-time jobs in the woodland.

On the Balmacara estate, on Loch Alsh, an estate owned by the National Trust, eight new crofts have been created out of farmland, bringing the total number of crofts up to twelve. Two Crofter Forestry Schemes are in operation. Crofters can augment their income by jobs available locally at the naval base, on the railway, at fish farms and hotels. The area is rich in wildlife, and many crofters here, and in the eight neighbouring crofting townships, are involved in the Rural Stewardship scheme, whereby grant aid can be given to those who take measures to help wildlife by adjusting harvesting dates, banning chemical sprays and so on. The combination of traditional crofting ways and modern land management makes for a sustainable, environmentally friendly set-up.

The Crofting Development Plan set out by the Crofters' Commission aims to encourage investment in croft land to support active crofting. Supplies of locally produced food, full and part-time employment, opportunities for small businesses, a healthy environment, local culture, and resources for the community, all these benefits accrue from the active use of croft land.

Of great importance in a crofting area, which depends largely on the use of the common grazing, is the establishment of a grazing committee. Training is given to clerks and assessors in the management of the grazings. Livestock and sheep stock clubs help to ensure the benefits of co-operative stock management, with appropriate stocking rates, organising the husbandry activities of gathering, dipping, shearing and so on. Shareholders in the grazings meet regularly and may consider plans for alternative uses of part of the area, perhaps for housing, woodland or environmental projects.

Crofter forestry is developing as a productive use of land. It is, of course a long-term asset. Shelter belts are of obvious benefit, as is the use of felled timber for fencing and other constructive purposes. Trees also create habitats for wildlife.

Environmental schemes in crofting areas include peatland management in Caithness, Sutherland and the Western Isles, and corncrake management in several of the Western Isles, to safeguard the populations of these breeding birds. For all these schemes grant aid is available.

Machinery rings and tool clubs can ensure that items too costly for individual purchase can be shared by a community.

Marketing is of vital importance in boosting croft income. Markets are now well established in towns not far from crofting areas. They provide an outlet for produce of all kinds which will satisfy the current demand for quality food grown in traditional ways, much of it organically. Presentation is important in the marketing of produce, as it is in livestock marketing, where grooming, marking and batching for size, type and quality makes the beasts attractive to buyers. Hand-crafted goods also sell well at the markets.

There are today about 17,000 registered crofts, comprising 10-12,000 crofting households. A new Crofter's Act is in the offing. Proposals under discussion may include measures for simplifying procedures, eliminating 'red tape', making for more flexibility in the assignation of tenancies and allowing for diversification in the management of land. In cases of disagreement, appeal can be made to the Land Court.

The Crofter's Foundation acts as a watchdog over the interests of the crofters, particularly those in fragile communities 'on the edge', whose special circumstances might not be recognised.

All in all, with the imaginative measures now being taken to promote the viability and the sustainability of crofts, it looks as though a return to many of the traditional ways is coming about. Communal activities, respect for the environment, sharing of resources, all these were part of the old way of life. A crofter in South Uist, when advised to manure his ground with seaweed instead of artificial fertiliser, remarked: 'It's what I've been doing all my life.' The return to organic cultivation and the current interest in the use of herbal remedies, these were a natural part of life in older times. Traditional music, the music of the ceilidh, step-dancing, all the expressions of the *joie de vivre* of people confident in the security of their communal life, these are back. And storytelling, holding a rapt audience of children and adults alike, is being re-enacted with the topics of the day—the modern magic of wind-power with its giant turbines striding the hills, the pictures of the planets flashed through space.

The old language, spoken, they say, in the Garden of Eden, that too, is alive in the schools and on the television. Gaelic-medium schools and playgroups are operating in many places. Gaelic programmes on television have a devoted following. Posts in the Islands are advertised as 'requiring an ability to communicate in Gaelic'.

Shinty, the great game that has been played since the earliest times, is thriving. It does not suffer from commercial exploitation, but is highly competitive and played with all the verve and gusto of the days of old clan battles.

Of course, with directives coming from Brussels affecting agriculture and fishing, adjustments have to be made to land use and food production everywhere. Crofting has to keep in step as it has always done. Community Management of Croft Land is what crofters have fought for over the years. This is what the Crofters' Commission says to the subject: 'Crofting is a strong and positive part of the present-day Highlands and Islands, helping sustain and build the area's economy, its rural communities and its environment. By using the land creatively, whether through traditional or innovative methods, crofters can advance the long-term viability of communities throughout the crofting areas. Community spirit, born out of self-help and confidence, is the key in helping communities overcome remoteness and natural disadvantage.'

With the Crofting Reform Bill set to keep crofting matters at the forefront of social and political thinking, and with the implementation of the Land Reform Act in operation, it seems there is to be a renewed movement of land reform towards the willing hands of those who long to work and care for it. The dreams of Màiri Mhór, John Murdoch and the countless fighters on the hillsides must now open out to reality.

FURTHER READING

Boyd, J. M. and Boyd, I. L. *The Hebrides: A Habitable Land*, Birlinn, Edinburgh, 1996.

Cameron, A. D. *Go Listen to the Crofters—The Napier Commission and Crofting a Century Ago*, Acair Ltd., Stornoway, 1990.

Carmichael, Alexander. *Carmina Gadelica*, Floris Books, Edinburgh, 1992.

Darling, F. Fraser. *Crofting Agriculture*, Oliver & Boyd Ltd., 1945.

Fenton, Alexander. *Scottish Country Life*, John Donald, Edinburgh, 1976.

Grant, I. F. *Highland Folk Ways*, Routledge and Kegan Paul, 1961.

Hunter, James. *The Claim of Crofting*, Mainstream Publishing, Edinburgh 1991.

Hunter, James. *The Making of the Crofting Community*, John Donald, Edinburgh, 1976.